ok 3

On Your Way

Building Basic Skills in English

Marjorie Fuchs

Cheryl Pavlik

Longman

Executive Editor: Joanne Dresner
Development Editor: Nancy Perry
Assistant Editor: Jari Flashner
Book Design: Levavi & Levavi, Inc.
Cover Illustration: Bill Schmidt
Production Director: Eduardo Castillo
Permissions and Photo Research: Jari Flashner, Esther Gottfried
Photo Credits: See page 124.
We wish to thank Penny Laporte and Lynn Luchetti for their contributions to this work.

We wish to thank the following artists:
Storyline artist: Roman Szolkowski.
Interior artists: Charlene Felker, Helen L. Granger, George Guzzi, Lydia Halverson, JAK Graphics, Mary Martylewski, Nancy Munger, Marcy Ramsey, Claudia Sargent.

On Your Way Student's Book 3

ISBN: 0–582–90762–4

Longman Inc.
95 Church St.
White Plains, N.Y. 10601

Associated companies:
Longman Group Ltd., London; Longman Cheshire Pty., Melbourne; Longman Paul Pty., Auckland; Copp Clark Pitman, Toronto; Pitman Publishing Inc., New York

Library of Congress Cataloging-in-Publication Data
(Revised for vol. 3)
Anger, Larry, 1942-
  On your way.
  Vol. 3 by Marjorie Fuchs, Cheryl Pavlik.
  Includes index.
  1. English language—Textbooks for foreign speakers.
I. Pavlik, Cheryl, 1949-   . II. Segal, Margaret,
1950-
PE1128.A53   1987   428.2'4   86-21524
ISBN 0-582-90760-8 (v. 1: pbk.)

Distributed in the United Kingdom by Longman Group Ltd., Longman House, Burnt Mill, Harlow, Essex CM20 2JE, England, and by associated companies, branches, and representatives throughout the world.

Printed in the U.S.A.

Consultants

JOSEPH BERKOWITZ
ESOL Program Coordinator
Miami Sunset Adult Education Center
Dade County
Miami, Florida

EILEEN K. BLAU
Associate Professor
Department of English
University of Puerto Rico
Mayaguez, Puerto Rico

CHERYL CREATORE
Curriculum Coordinator of ESL
Seneca Community College
Toronto, Ontario, Canada

JUDITH E. KLEEMAN
Manager Refugee Program
Houston Community College
Houston, Texas

JOANN LA PERLA
Director of Continuing Education and
    Community Services
Union County College
Cranford, New Jersey

VIRGINIA LoCASTRO
Lecturer
The University of Tsukuba
Japan

BARBARA MOTEN
Assistant Director - Project C3
Department of Adult Education
Detroit Public Schools
Detroit, Michigan

K. LYNN SAVAGE
Vocational ESL Resource Instructor
San Francisco Community College Centers
San Francisco, California

Contents

1 This is the newsroom of the Houston *Herald* daily newspaper. Angela Lentini, the editor, is welcoming Pete Gómez, a new reporter. Listen to their conversation.

1

ANGELA: Well, this is our newsroom, Pete.
PETE: I'm glad to see you're using computers.
ANGELA: We just started using them last year, and our reporters are happy with the change.

2

TOM: Except for me, Angela.
ANGELA: Pete, meet Tom Kirby, our sports reporter, and the only one who still prefers to use a typewriter.
TOM: How do you do, Pete?
PETE: Nice to meet you, Tom. You know, it's easier to do your stories over on the computer. You should try it some day.
TOM: I just don't like machines that can erase your work if the power goes out.

3

ANGELA: And this is Linda Smith. She usually covers politics, but right now she's working on something special.
LINDA: That's right. I'm doing a story about all those warehouse fires.
PETE: Do the police think it might be arson?
LINDA: Well, *I* think so. The fires always happen at night, and they spread very quickly. The whole building burns down before the firefighters can put the fire out. It sure sounds like the work of an arsonist to me.

2 Correct the information.

1. Pete is the reporters' boss.
2. Tom likes computers.
3. Linda thinks the fires are an accident.
4. The fires are easy to put out.
5. Arsonists put out fires.

3 Find a word or phrase in the conversation that means:

1. electricity
2. do again
3. reports on
4. likes better

4 Warm Up

Introduce two people.

A: *Sam, meet Bill. Bill works in my office.*
B: *It's a pleasure to meet you, Bill.*
A: Good to meet you too.

DEVELOP YOUR VOCABULARY

Have you met *Carlos*?
I'd like to introduce you to *Reiko*.
This is my *wife, Ingrid*.
. . .

Practice

A.

> Linda usually **writes** about politics.
> Right now she**'s writing** about something special.

Usually

1 The pictures show what Linda Smith usually does and what she is doing now. Ask and answer questions about Linda's habits.

1. arson / politics

A: Does Linda usually *write about arson?*
B: No, she doesn't. She usually *writes about politics.*
OR
A: Does Linda usually *write about politics?*
B: Yes, she does. But now she's *writing about arson.*

2. office / home
3. full meal / sandwich

Find three more differences between the pictures and talk about them.

Now

2 Angela Lentini is introducing Pete Gómez to some other members of the news staff. Listen and write what she says about each person.

1. Cathy Wilson

She *writes* _____.

2. Brad Kimball

He _____

3. Minh Tran

He _____.

3 Pete Gómez is writing a letter to his girlfriend, Suzanne. Complete his letter with the simple present or the present progressive form of the verb.

> **Note:** These verbs are not usually used in the progressive form.
>
> be   like, love, want
> have (=possession), own   need
> have to   seem
> know, think

The Houston Herald

Dear Suzanne,

I'm typing _____ this letter because
   1. type

I _____ late at the office. I _____
   2. work   3. write

a story for the Sunday paper about the next election.

I really _____ it here. The other reporters
           4. like

_____ very nice. One of them, the sports
   5. seem

reporter, Tom Kirby, _____ me find a
                           6. help

bigger apartment. Michael and I really

_____ more space.
   7. need

   The staff here _____ harder than
                        8. work

we did at the Dallas Star. Tom says that he often

_____ late, and another reporter,
   9. stay

Linda Smith, _____ in every Saturday.
              10. come

I _____ it's going to be hard, but I
   11. know

_____ I can learn a lot here.
   12. think

   Well, I should get back to work. I

_____ to finish this article before I go
   13. want

home. I really miss you and can't wait to see you

next week.

                              Love,
                              Pete

P.S. Any news from Montreal? How's your family
doing?

4 Write about a friend's or relative's habits. Then tell a classmate.

1. My friend _____ usually _____.
              (name)

2. He (She) never _____.

3. He (She) _____ at 6:30.

4. It's 5:00 now. I think _____.
                          (friend's name)

B.

Pete **can** use a computer. Tom **can't**.
Tom **should** learn to use one. He **shouldn't** be afraid to.
He **might** like it. He **might not.**

Note: We do not contract *might not.*

1 Talk about the pictures. Use the words below them.

1. Angela can use a computer.

1. can   2. should   3. can't   4. might   5. shouldn't

2 Linda Smith and Tom Kirby are having lunch. Read the sentences below. Then listen to their conversation and choose the correct answers.

1. Linda thinks she ___*might*___ see a movie.
    might / should

2. Tom thinks she _____ see a Spanish movie.
    should / shouldn't

3. Tom _____ understand Spanish.
    can / might

4. Linda says she _____ understand a film in Spanish.
    might not / can't

5. Tom thinks she _____ understand a lot.
    might / might not

6. Linda thinks she _____ work more tonight.
    should / might

7. Tom thinks Linda _____ work so much.
    shouldn't / can't

8. He thinks she _____ have a good time.
    should / can't

3 Talk about someone who doesn't like his or her job.

A: *My sister* really hates *her* job.
B: Then *she* should find a new one. Can *she type?*
A: Yes, *she* can.
B: Why doesn't *she* look for a job as *a computer operator? She* might like that better.

OR

A: No, *she* can't.
B: Hmm. Then *she* can't be *a computer operator.* Well, can *she . . . ?*

Student B can use these ideas:

drive . . . taxi driver, chauffeur
sew . . . tailor
speak two languages . . . bilingual secretary, translator
work with numbers . . . cashier, bookkeeper
cook . . . chef, caterer

C.

The firefighters couldn't	**put out** the fire. **put** the fire **out**. **put** it **out**.

Other separable two-word verbs:

bring back	find out	look up
call up	get back	pick up
do over	hand in	point out
drop off	look over	think over

Note: You have to separate these verbs when you use pronouns.
You cannot say:
The firefighters couldn't ~~put out it.~~

1   Choose the sentences that describe the pictures.

1. ____ Angela's pointing out a mistake.
2. _a_ Linda's looking up a word.
3. ____ Minh's calling up his wife.
4. ____ Angela's looking over an article.
5. ____ Pete's dropping off his son.

2   Now use a pronoun in each sentence like this:

Linda's looking it up.

3   Angela Lentini is telling Pete Gómez about procedures for writing an article at the *Herald*. Complete the sentences. Be sure to put the pronouns in the correct place.

1. The reporters have to _hand in their stories_ by 3:00.
   hand in (their stories)

2. Then the editors _____ .
   look over (them)

   They _____ .
   point out (problems)

4. Sometimes the reporters have to _____ .
   do over (their stories)

5. Then they have to _____ by 6:00.
   bring back (them)

6

4 Now ask and answer questions about procedures at the *Herald*.

1. When / have to hand in stories
A: When do the reporters have to hand in their stories?
B: They have to hand them in by 3:00.

2. Who / look over the stories
3. What / point out
4. What / reporters sometimes have to do
5. When / have to bring back revised stories

5 Ask a friend about his or her schoolwork.

A: Do you ever *look up words in the dictionary?*
B: Yes, I *look them up when I don't understand them.*
   OR   No, I never *look them up.*

You can use these ideas:

hand in assignments late
look over your homework
call up classmates for help
point out other students' mistakes

Note: Not all two-word verbs can be separated:
Look at the book.→ **Look at** it.
They**'re talking about** Angela. → They**'re talking about** her.
He always **waits for** the bus. → He always **waits for** it.

PUT IT ALL TOGETHER
Linda called Pete to tell him about another fire. Listen to their conversation and decide which story will be in tomorrow's newspaper.

The Hous

Fire Kills 5, Injures 50
1

The Hous

Fire Destroys School
2

The Houston Herald

Arsonist Burns Factory Down
3

The Houston Herald

Firefighters Save Building
4

ON YOUR OWN
Discuss these questions with your classmates.

1 Do you usually read the newspaper? If so, which one(s)? What's your favorite section?

2 How do the newspapers from your country compare to the newspapers where you are now living? Consider the cost, size, ads, editorials, special sections, and number and type of photographs.

Reading

1 **Predicting. What kind of article is this? What helped you to recognize it? What kind of information do you expect to find in an article of this kind?**

The Houston Herald

Dear Dr. Cousins

Dear Dr. Cousins:

My husband and I immigrated to the United States five years ago. Now he° wants to go back
(5) to our° country. He says that he doesn't feel comfortable in this country. He says that there are more opportunities available back home. In a way this is true
(10) for him°, because in all this time my husband has refused to learn to speak English. I think he's really angry because my English is much better than his°
(15) and I have found a good job as a bank teller.

What can I do? I don't want to go back. My children and I like our life here; it's much easier
(20) than our life back home was. My husband just doesn't remember how bad things are in our country. We fight about this° almost every day. What
(25) should I do?

DON'T WANT TO GO

Dear Don't:

You have a difficult problem; however, it's not an uncommon
(30) one°. Maybe you should go back to your country for a month. Perhaps your husband will decide that life here° is easier and want to come back
(35) and give the United States another chance.

However, you should realize that he might decide that he really wants to stay there°.
(40) Perhaps you and your children will see that life there isn't as bad as you all° think. Your ability to speak English is probably valuable in your country too. It
(45) might help you find an even better job there. Good luck!

DR. COUSINS

---

2 **Comprehension. Answer the questions.**

Who . . .

1. wants to leave the United States?
2. can't speak English well?
3. likes the United States?
4. works as a bank teller?

5. thinks they should take a trip home?
6. may be able to find a better job outside the United States?

3 **Understanding pronouns. We often use pronouns so that we don't have to repeat information. Find each of these pronouns in the letters and say what they refer to:**

Letter 1		Letter 2	
Line 4:	he	Line 30:	one
5:	our	33:	here
10:	him	39:	there
14:	his	42:	you all
24:	this		

4 **Discussion. What do you think? Discuss these questions with your classmates.**

1. Do you think Dr. Cousins gave the woman good ~~advice~~
2. What would you advise her to do?

Writing

Skill: Expressing contrast or contradiction
Task: Writing a letter describing a problem

1 We often use *however* instead of *but*, especially in formal speech and in writing.

She wanted to immigrate, but she couldn't get a visa.
She wanted to immigrate; however, she couldn't get a visa.
OR She wanted to immigrate. However, she couldn't get a visa.

Rewrite these sentences using *however*. Write each sentence two ways.

1. We found an apartment, but it won't be available until June 1.
2. The students didn't understand all the words, but they were able to read the article.
3. Miguel wants to go home, but his wife and children are happy here.
4. Nguyen wants to work, but he can't find a good job.
5. There are many opportunities in this country, but there are also many difficulties.

2 Complete these statements.

1. All students need to do homework; however, . . .
2. Wives and husbands should talk over their differences; however, . . .
3. It's good to be ambitious. However, . . .
4. Immigrating to a new country can be exciting; however, . . .
5. Children should obey their parents. However, . . .

3 Write a letter to Dr. Cousins similar to the one on page 8. Do not sign your real name. Give the letter to your teacher. Your teacher will give you another student's letter so that you can answer it. Try to use *however* in your letter and in your response.

For pronunciation exercises for Unit 1, see page

2 It Looks Like Arson

1 Linda Smith is at the police station talking to an investigator about the fire. Listen to their conversation.

1

LINDA: Do you think it was arson, Officer Brady?

BRADY: Well, I've been in the arson division since 1965, and it looks like arson to me. By the way, what were *you* doing down there on a Sunday afternoon?

LINDA: Actually, I went to meet an informant.

BRADY: How long have you been a reporter?

LINDA: For about five years. Why?

BRADY: I read your article in today's *Herald.* You're very good. Great photographs too.

LINDA: Thanks. Our photographer Minh Tran is excellent.

BRADY: Well, be careful. Things might get dangerous.

2

TOM: What did the police say?

LINDA: They think it *was* arson. They also wanted to know why I was at the scene of the fire.

MINH: Why *were* you there?

LINDA: To meet Bill Thomas, a neighbor of mine. He had some information for me, but he didn't show up.

TOM: How long did you wait?

LINDA: About a half an hour. Then I saw the smoke.

3

LINDA: Linda Smith.

ALICE: Linda, this is Alice Thomas. Billy's in the hospital. He was hit by a car.

LINDA: What? I'll be right there.

2 Say *That's right* or *That's wrong.*

1. Officer Brady works for the fire department.
2. Officer Brady thinks the fire was arson.
3. Linda didn't meet the informant.
4. Linda has been a reporter longer than Officer Brady has been a police officer.
5. Alice Thomas was in a car accident.

4 Warm Up

Think of something you know about a classmate and ask him or her about it.

A: Why did you *sell your car?*

B: Because I wanted to *buy a new one.*

3 Find a word or phrase in the conversation that means:

1. location
2. arrive
3. a person who gives information

Student A can use these ideas:

register for this class	give up *cigarettes*
go to *the optician*	become *a taxi driver*
immigrate to this country	

—Practice—

A.

Minh **has** Minh's	**lived** in the U.S.A.	**since**	1975. he left Vietnam.
		for a long time.	

1 Talk about Minh's life. Use *for* and *since*.

1. Minh has lived in the United States since 1975.

1. live / 1975

2. be / a long time

3. have / he came to this country

4. work / 1984

5. know / 3 years

2 Linda is at the hospital talking to Alice Thomas. Complete their conversation with *for* or *since*.

LINDA: Have you seen Bill yet?

ALICE: No, he's been unconscious __*since*__ they brought him in. The doctors have been
        1

with him _____ more than two hours now.
        2

LINDA: Don't worry. People are often unconscious after they've had an accident. Did the police

tell you what happened?

ALICE: No, they don't know. They've only spoken to one witness _____ Bill's been here. Oh,
                                                                    3

Linda, he's been so happy _____ he started school. He's studied every night. And
                            4

he hasn't been in trouble _____ a long time.
                            5

LINDA: I'm sure he'll be all right, Alice.

3 Linda is telling Pete about Bill Thomas's life. Listen to their conversation and write Bill's age for each event and his age now.

Event	Bill's Age
1. family moved next to Linda	4
2. father died	____
3. police arrested him for the first time	____
4. quit school	____
5. went to prison for arson	____
6. got out of prison	____
7. became a mechanic	____
8. got his high school diploma	____
9. started studying computer programming at Houston Business Institute	____
Bill's age now	____

Now use the information to ask and answer questions about Bill's life. Begin with _How long_.

1. Linda / know Bill's family

A: How long has Linda known Bill's family?
B: For 17 years.   OR   Since Bill was four.

2. Bill's mother / be a widow
3. Bill / be out of prison
4. he / be a mechanic
5. Bill / have his high school diploma
6. he / study at Houston Business Institute

4 Ask a classmate about his or her life.

A: How long have you _been a student here?_
B: Oh, for _about two months._   OR   Since _February._

DEVELOP YOUR VOCABULARY

for:

a long while	two quarters
quite some time	the past _two years_
only a short time	ages
one semester(s)	. . .

Student A can use these ideas:

wear _glasses_	work for _the phone company_
have _that jacket_	speak _Spanish_
live in _Chicago_	

B.

When **did** Pete **move** to Texas?	**In 1977.** Thirteen years **ago.**
How long **did** he **live** in Dallas before he moved to Houston?	**For** thirteen years.

| How long **has** he **lived** in Houston? | **For** two months.
Since March. |

1 Pete is asking Linda about Angela Lentini. Listen to their conversation and decide if Angela completed the action or is still doing it.

	Completed past	Present
1. teach journalism		✓
2. be married		
3. live in the suburbs		

	Completed past	Present
4. live in town		
5. ski		
6. play the piano		

2 Before he got his job at the Houston *Herald,* Pete Gómez had an interview with Angela Lentini. Look at Pete's résumé and the notes that Angela took during the interview.

born in L.A.
moved to Dallas '77

Peter L. Gómez
2416 Sunset Boulevard
Houston, Texas 77005
(713) 327-2719

bilingual Spanish/English (spoke both languages at home)

Experience:

1977–1990   Dallas Star — reporter

'87–'88 studied French

moved to Houston March 1, 1990
* Start work here May 7, 1990

1975–1976   University of California at Los Angeles — editor of college newspaper

1979–present member of Writers' Society

Education:

1972–1976   B.A. Journalism, University of California at Los Angeles

Now find out about Pete's life. Pretend the date is May 9, 1990, and ask and answer questions like these:

A: How long *did he live in Dallas?*
B: He *lived there for thirteen years.*

A: How long *has he lived in Houston?*
B: He's *lived there for two months (since March).*

Ask about these facts:

go to UCLA
speak Spanish
work for Dallas *Star*
write for Houston *Herald*
study French
be member of Writers' Society
be editor of college newspaper
live in Texas

3 Cathy Wilson interviewed the owner of a Japanese restaurant in Houston. Read the first part of the interview and complete it with the simple past or present perfect form of the verbs.

The Houston Herald

Eating Ethnic in Houston   PART 3: *JAPAN*

by Cathy Wilson

Cathy: You __were born__ in Japan. When
                    1. be born
_____ you _____ to
                                    2. decide
come to the United States?

Yamoto: My husband's an American, so I
_____ to the United States when
            3. come
I got married in 1970. We _____ in
                                            4. live
Houston for the past ten years.

Cathy: How long ago _____ you
_____ Rikyu?
            5. open

Yamoto: Oh, we _____ here for almost
                          6. be
four years.

Cathy: _____ Rikyu immediately
                  7. be
successful?

Yamoto: Yes. It _____ incredible.
                          8. be
People _____ coming immediately.
              9. start

Another busy lunch hour at Rikyu.

I have one customer who _____
                                              10. eat
here one night a week since we opened.

Cathy: That's wonderful. _____ you
_____ any experience in
            11. have
the restaurant business before
you _____ ?
          12. start

Yamoto: Yes. My father _____ a chef in
                                        13. be
Tokyo for thirty years.

CONT. P. B6 COL. 2

---

4 Complete this chart about yourself or someone you know.

NAME:	
Past	**Present**
address	....
....	....
occupation	....
marital status	....
interests	....

Now exchange charts with a classmate and interview him or her. Ask and answer questions like these with *how long*:

(past) How long did you live at _____ ?
(present) How long have you lived at _____ ?

C.

Why did Linda go to the factory?	She went **to meet** an informant.
Why does Minh wear a helmet?	**To protect** his head.

1 Match the questions in column A with the responses in column B to give reasons for these characters' actions.

A

1. _b_ Why did Linda go to the factory?
2. ____ Why did Pete move to Houston?
3. ____ Why did Tom look at the newspaper?
4. ____ Why is Pete going to Dallas next weekend?
5. ____ Why did Bill's mother call up the *Herald?*
6. ____ Why does Angela look over the articles?
7. ____ Why did Pete stay at work late?
8. ____ Why does Minh wear a helmet?

B

a. To look for mistakes.
b. To meet an informant.
c. To finish an article.
d. To get a better job.
e. To see his girlfriend, Suzanne.
f. To protect his head.
g. To tell Linda about the accident.
h. To find a good movie.

2 Ask a classmate why he or she signed up for this class.

A: Why did you sign up for this class?
B: To *improve my English.* How about you?
A: . . .

Student B can use these ideas:

meet new people	get out of the house
prepare for an exam	make new friends
get a promotion at work	

Just for Fun

3 What can you use these objects for? Think of as many uses as possible for each of these items. Use your imagination!

1. You can use bricks ⎰ to make a wall.
                        ⎱ to draw a rectangle.
                          to hold papers down.
                          . . .

1. bricks

2. rubber bands

3. straw

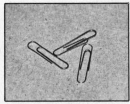

4. paper clips

5. pot holders

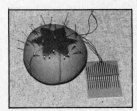

6. pins and needles

Life Skills

Health care

1 When Bill Thomas arrived at the hospital emergency room, the doctors knew who to call because Bill had an identification card in his wallet. Look at Bill's card and then fill out one of your own.

> **MEDICAL I.D.**
>
> Patient's Name: _Bill Thomas_   Date of Birth: _5/14/69_
>
> Address: _6411 Rolling Brook Lane, Houston Tx, 77038_
>
> Tel.: (Home) _225-7390_   (Business) _255-0621_
>
> In Emergency Notify: (Name) _Alice Thomas_
>
> (Relationship) _Mother_   (Tel.) _858-7390_
>
> Medical Problems: _none_
>
> Present Medication: _none_
>
> Known Drug Allergies: _Penicillin_

2 Linda Smith is calling the hospital to get some information about Bill. Listen and complete the conversation.

OPERATOR: City Hospital.

LINDA: Hello, I'd like some information about _____ _____ . He's a new patient at your
                                    1   2

     _____ .
     3

OPERATOR: One minute. I'll connect you to the nurses' station on his _____ .
                                                        4

    (The operator rings the nurses' station.)

NURSE: _____ floor, Nurse Spencer.
    5

LINDA: Hello. This is _____ _____ . Can you please tell me the _____ of Bill Thomas?
                               6   7   8

NURSE: Are you related to the _____ ?
                          9

LINDA: I'm a close _____ of the family.
                  10

NURSE: I see. Well, _____ condition is listed as critical.
                    11

LINDA: Oh. Can you tell me what the visiting _____ are?
                                    12

NURSE: They're from _____ to _____ in the _____ and _____ to _____ at night.
                      13   14   15   16   17

LINDA: And what _____ is he in?
                    18

NURSE: _____ . It's on the fifth floor, _____ Wing. But only _____ can see him now.
      19   20   21

LINDA: Thank you.

3 Here is a list of some other patients at City Hospital.

NAME	ROOM	FLOOR	WING	CONDITION	VISITING HOURS
Johnson, Tommy	3021	3	Children's	guarded	8:30 A.M.-8:30 P.M. parents and grandparents only
McKormick, Karen	recovery	8	East	critical	none
Rifkin, Lynn	1121	11	Maternity	good	11:30 A.M.-1:00 P.M. 7:00-8:15 P.M. 24 hours fathers
Rivera, Juanita	intensive care	8	East	stable	1:30-3:30 P.M. 6:00-8:30 P.M.
Shakter, David	906	9	West	fair	1:00-4:00 P.M. 6:00-8:30 P.M.

Now roleplay phone conversations like the one in Exercise 2. Use the information in the list above.

4 Dr. Valdez is asking Mrs. Thomas some questions about Bill's medical history.

DR. VALDEZ: Has Bill ever had a concussion?
MRS. THOMAS: No, he hasn't.
DR. VALDEZ: Has he ever had pneumonia?
MRS. THOMAS: Yes. He had pneumonia five years ago.

DEVELOP YOUR VOCABULARY

anemia
hemorrhaging
convulsions
a high fever
shortness of breath

asthma
heart disease
allergic reaction to a drug
. . .

Now roleplay a similar situation with a classmate. Give information about yourself or someone you know.

ON YOUR OWN
Discuss these questions with your classmates.

1 Have you ever been to a hospital emergency room? When should you go to one?

2 Do you have health insurance? If so, what does your insurance cover (routine doctors' visits, second opinions, hospitalization, surgery)?

3 How does health insurance here compare to health insurance in your country?

For pronunciation exercises for Unit 2, see page 112.

REVIEW 1

45/45

1 Read the conversation on page 2 again and complete these sentences with the present progressive or the simple present form of the verbs.

1. Angela *is introducing* Pete to the staff of the
   introduce
   Houston *Herald*.

2. Angela ___is___ the editor of the *Herald*.
   be

3. Pete *doesn't know* the *Herald* staff.
   know—neg.

4. In picture 2, Tom and Peter *are shaking* hands.
   shake

5. Tom *isn't wearing* a jacket today.
   wear—neg.

6. Tom always *writes* his stories on a typewriter.
   write

7. Tom *doesn't like* computers.
   like—neg.

8. Pete *thinks* computers are easy to use.
   think

9. Linda usually *covers* politics, but right now
   cover
   she *is writing* a story about a fire.
   write

10. The police *need* more information about
    need
    some warehouse fires.

2 Match the questions in column A with the responses in column B.

	A		B
1.	_c_	What do you do?	a. Nice to meet you.
2.	_a_	How do you do?	b. Yes, I am.
3.	_e_	What are you doing?	c. I'm a writer.
4.	_f_	Do you do a lot of work?	d. Fine, thanks.
5.	_d_	How are you doing?	e. I'm writing a book.
6.	_b_	Are you doing a lot of work?	f. Yes, I do.

Now answer the questions in column A with your own information.

3 Complete the conversation with *can/can't*, *should/shouldn't* or *might/might not*.

PETE: You *shouldn't* climb on the table. You *might* fall. Why don't you go and do your
          1   2
          homework?

MICHAEL: I started it, but I *can't* finish it. It's too hard. *Can* you help me with it?
          3   4

PETE: Sure. I'll help you with it later, after I finish my work. But it *might not* be before
          5
          10:00. I'm very busy.

MICHAEL: OK. I have a test next week, and I'm afraid I *might* fail.
          6

PETE: Don't worry. I'm sure you *can* pass. Just study more. You really *should* study
          7   8
          a few hours every day.

MICHAEL: You're right, Dad. It *might* be difficult, but I'm sure I *can* do it.
          9   10

4 Make sentences with these words.

1. over have to do you'll it
   You'll have to do it over.

2. bring please back it 7:00 by
   Please, bring it back by 7:00.

3. out it the firefighters put quickly
   The firefighters put it out quickly.

4. forgot he off them turn to
   He forgot to turn them off.

5. when I'll you call up arrive I
   I'll call you up when I arrive.

6. outside me he theater picked the up
   He picked me up outside the theater.

18

✗ 5   Answer each question with a sentence from Exercise 4.

1. A: Where did you meet Bill last night?
   B: _____ 6 _____
2. A: Why are all the lights on?
   B: _____ 4 _____
3. A: Was the fire very bad?
   B: No. _____ 3 _____

4. A: When will you be back?
   B: I'm not sure. _____ 5 _____
5. A: Did you like my story?
   B: I'm sorry. _____ 1 _____
6. A: When will you need your car?
   B: _____ 2 _____

6   Can you remember the story? Make true statements by combining the two parts of the sentences with *for* or *since*.

1. _f._   Linda has been a reporter _for_
2. ___   Pete has worked at the *Herald* _____
3. ___   Linda has been friends with Bill's family _____
4. ___   Bill has been in trouble _____
5. ___   Angela has lived in Houston _____
6. ___   Angela hasn't skied _____

a. he was twelve.
b. her accident.
c. they moved into her apartment building.
d. she left Canada.
e. a few days.
f. five years.

1. Linda has been a reporter for five years.

7   Look at the time line of Linda's life. Write questions in the simple past or the present perfect and answer them.

1981		1985	1986	1987	1990
	attended University of Chicago		left Chicago	started at *Herald*/met Minh	
		worked at Chicago *Sun*	worked at Houston *Chronicle*		

1. How long / live in Houston

How long has Linda lived in Houston?
Since 1986. / For *five* years.

2. When / move from Chicago

3. Where / go to college
4. How long / work at the *Herald*
5. When / meet Minh
6. Where / work in Houston
7. Where / work in Chicago

✗ 8   Change the answers from *because* to *to* + verb.

1. A: Why did Alice go to the store?
   B: Because she needed some milk. (buy)

To buy some milk.

2. A: Why is Bill studying computer programming?
   B: Because he would like a better job. (get)

To get a better job

3. A: Why does Angela wear glasses?
   B: Because she can't see well.   So that she can see better. ✓ To see better.

4. A: Why does Michael have to go to the language lab?
   B: Because he needs to practice pronunciation.   To practice pronunciation.

5. A: Why did Suzanne join the French Club?
   B: Because she wanted to meet new people.

To meet new people. ✓

Just for Fun

✗ 9   Which word doesn't belong?

1. photographers   editors   reporters   (informants)
2. politics   (buildings)   sports   health and food
3. robbery   arson   murder   (accident)

4. eraser   (computer)   typewriter   pencil
5. journalism   (arson)   history   mathematics
6. article   headline   editorial   (conversation)

3 Who Turned Out the Lights?

1 The Houston *Herald* reporters are working hard to finish their stories for tomorrow's edition of the paper. Listen to their conversation.

1

TOM: I tried to reach you last night, Linda.

LINDA: I was at the hospital with Bill's mother.

TOM: Have the police found out what happened?

LINDA: Yes. It was a hit-and-run accident. Bill was walking on Bank Street when a car came up on the sidewalk, hit him and took off.

TOM: Were there any witnesses?

LINDA: Yes, but they didn't see the license plate.

TOM: It doesn't sound like an accident to me. Bill used to have some pretty bad friends. Do you think he's in trouble again?

LINDA: I'm not sure.

2

ANGELA: I'm leaving for Dallas now. Linda, I asked Brad to get you that information you need about the warehouses. Have you finished the Cooper article, Tom?

TOM: Not yet. I'll show it to you when you get back on Friday.

3

LINDA: Speaking of getting back—I should get back to work.

TOM: Hey! Who turned out the lights? Look outside, the whole city's dark!

LINDA: And all my work just disappeared from the computer.

TOM: See, a typewriter still has some advantages.

2 Correct the information.

1. Linda wanted to talk to Tom last night.
2. Linda was at the hospital alone last night.
3. Bill was crossing the street when a car hit him.
4. The witnesses saw the license plate.
5. Angela is going to Dallas on Friday.

4 Warm Up

Tell a classmate what you did last night, and he or she will change the subject, like this:

A: I had dinner with friends last night.

B: That reminds me . . . have you talked to Maria lately?

3 Find a word or phrase in the conversation that means:

1. return
2. have gotten information
3. people who see a crime or an accident
4. left quickly

DEVELOP YOUR VOCABULARY

Speaking of { restaurants / Linda / movies
shopping / going to the store

By the way, . . .

. . .

Practice

A.

What **was** Tom **doing**	when the lights went out?	He **was typing** an article.
What **did** Tom **do**		He **looked out** the window.

1 Talk about what people were doing at the time of the blackout and what they did right after the lights went out.

1. A: What was Tom doing when the lights went out?
   B: He was typing an article.
   A: What did Tom do when the lights went out?
   B: He looked out the window.

1

2

3

4

5

2 Pete is talking on the phone to his girlfriend, Suzanne. He's telling her about the blackout. Listen and complete their conversation.

SUZANNE: I heard about the blackout on the news. Are you and Michael OK?

PETE: Oh, we're both fine.

SUZANNE: What _____ _____ _____ when the lights went out?
                                 1   2   3

PETE: I _____ _____ someone about the next election.
           4   5

SUZANNE: Oh? _____ _____ you _____ then?
                  6   7   8

PETE: I _____ _____ a cassette recorder with batteries, so we just
         9   10

      _____ the interview.
        11

SUZANNE: And what about Michael? Where was he _____ _____ _____
                                     12   13   14

      _____ _____ ?
        15   16

PETE: He _____ _____ his homework at home. When the lights went out, he
         17   18

    just _____ _____ a flashlight and _____ .
        19   20   21

3 Alice Thomas was at the hospital when the blackout occurred. Read what she wrote in a letter to her sister and complete it with the simple past tense or the past progressive tense.

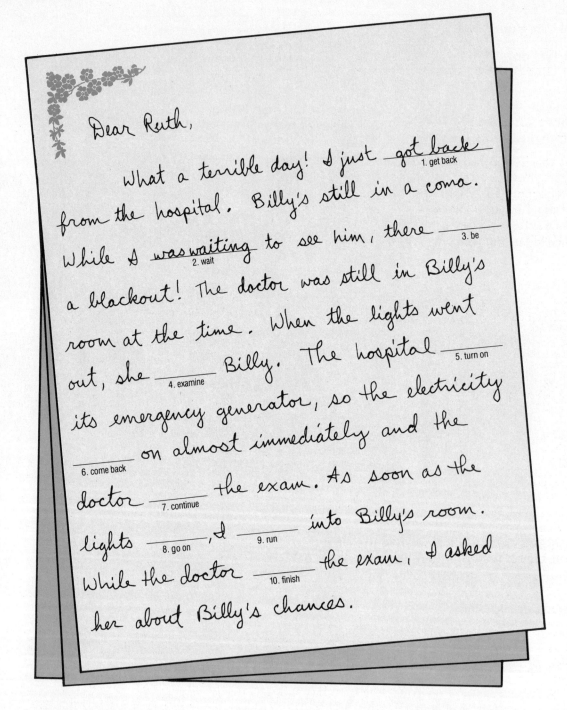

Dear Ruth,

What a terrible day! I just __got back__
1. get back
from the hospital. Billy's still in a coma.
While I __was waiting__ to see him, there ____
2. wait   3. be
a blackout! The doctor was still in Billy's
room at the time. When the lights went
out, she ____ Billy. The hospital ____
4. examine   5. turn on
____ on almost immediately and the
6. come back
doctor ____ the exam. As soon as the
7. continue
lights ____, I ____ into Billy's room.
8. go on   9. run
While the doctor ____ the exam, I asked
10. finish
her about Billy's chances.

4 Talk about the first time you met someone special.

A: What were you doing the first time you met *your girlfriend?*
B: I was *standing at a bus stop.*
A: What did you do (say)?
B: I *asked her for the time.*

Student A can use these ideas:

best friend *Alicia*	husband
fiancé (fiancée)	wife
boyfriend	

B.

Before her accident, Angela **used to ski,** but now she doesn't.

Did Angela **use to paint?**	No, she **didn't.**

She **didn't use to paint.**

1 Find six things in Angela's past that are different from her life now. Talk about them like this:

Angela used to *ski*, but now she *paints*.

2 Can you remember the story? Complete the sentences with *didn't use to* or *used to* + verb.

1. Pete / work on weekends at the Dallas *Star*

Pete didn't use to work on weekends at the Dallas *Star*.

2. Bill / get into trouble a lot
3. Linda / write her stories on a typewriter
4. Angela / live in Toronto
5. Minh / ride a motorcycle in Vietnam
6. Alice Thomas / be married
7. the Houston *Herald* / have computers

3 The Houston *Herald* is an old paper. Use the cues and the chart to ask and answer questions about the *Herald* in 1910 and now.

1910	Now
15 employees	110 employees
reporters used typewriters	reporters use computers
no women	1/2 staff are women
cost 5¢	costs 30¢
10 pages	40 pages
weekly	daily

1. How many people / work there
A: How many people used to work there?
B: Fifteen.
A: How many people work there now?
B: 110.

2. How / reporters / write stories
3. How many women / work there
4. How much / it cost
5. How many pages / it have
6. How often / it come out

4 Talk about how your life has changed since you moved to this country.

A: Has your life changed a lot since you moved here?
B: Oh, yes. I used to *visit my relatives often, but now I never see them.* How about you?
A: I didn't use to *like American food, but I do now.*

5 Reminisce with a classmate.

A: Who do you remember best from your childhood?
B: *My uncle. He* always used to *tell me stories.*

C.

What did Angela **want Brad to do?**	She **wanted him to get** the information for Linda and **to help** Pete Gómez.

1 Before Angela left for Dallas, she told Brad what she wanted people at the *Herald* to do. Brad made a list. Listen to the conversation and write the name of the person next to each job.

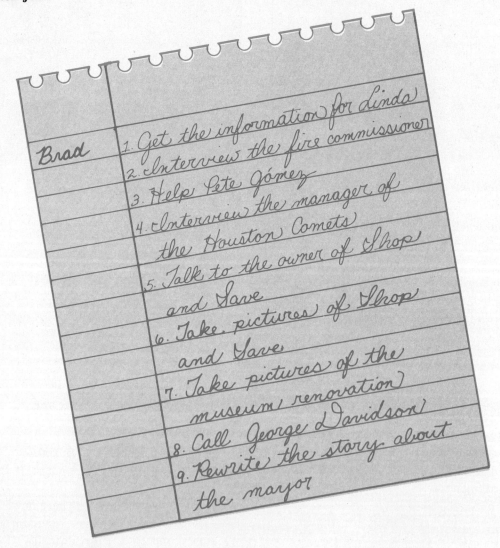

Brad
1. Get the information for Linda
2. Interview the fire commissioner
3. Help Pete Gómez
4. Interview the manager of the Houston Comets
5. Talk to the owner of Shop and Save
6. Take pictures of Shop and Save
7. Take pictures of the museum renovation
8. Call George Davidson
9. Rewrite the story about the mayor

Now talk about what Angela wanted her staff to do.

1. A: What did Angela want Brad to do?
   B: She wanted him to get the information for Linda and to help Pete Gómez.

2 Make sentences about the people with the words below each note or picture.

1. Angela wanted Brad to get Linda the information.

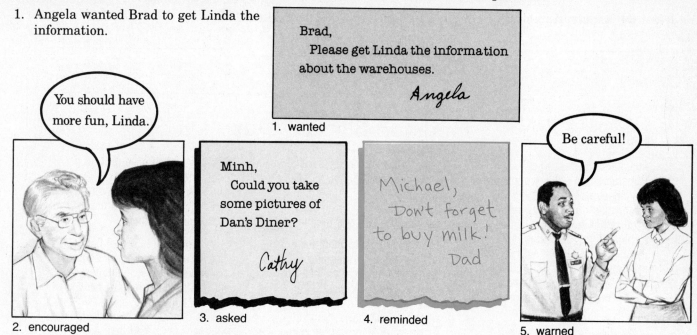

1. wanted

2. encouraged

3. asked

4. reminded

5. warned

3 Think of something you asked someone to do this week.

A: I asked *my sister* to *call me at 9:00.*
B: Why did you want *her* to do that?
A: I wanted *her* to *wake me up.*

PUT IT ALL TOGETHER
Bill Thomas has come out of his coma. Officer Brady is asking him some questions.
Read the notes below. Then listen to the conversation and choose the notes that Officer
Brady made.

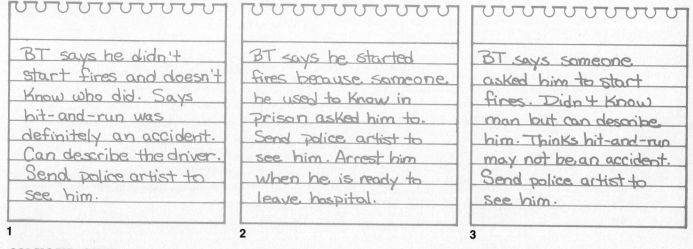

ON YOUR OWN
Think about Tom's feelings about computers and discuss these questions with your classmates.

1 Have you ever used a computer? Do you like them? Why or why not?

2 How have computers changed people's lives? What are some advantages of computers? Disadvantages?

Reading

1   Read the article. As you read, make a list of the words you don't know.

The Houston Herald

Houston Blacked Out

HOUSTON—Almost all of Houston stood still last night as the city experienced its biggest power blackout. The blackout (5) occurred at 7:38 P.M. when a turbine at the East Texas Power Plant blew up. Power was restored to most of the city within three hours, and a spokesperson for (10) East Texas Power said all areas would have power by noon.

As soon as the power went out, repairpersons from East Texas Power rushed to the power (15) plant to try to repair the damage.

Police Chief Michaelson called in extra police officers to take care of the massive traffic problems that occurred when the (20) traffic lights stopped functioning.

Local hospitals were not affected because they have emergency generators; however, the blackout did cause some (25) other unusual events. The power went out just as the Houston Astros were starting their game, and the 38,000 spectators were led out of the stadium in the (30) dark. In the Conroy Building,

Sarah Marsden gave birth to a baby girl in the elevator while she was waiting for rescuers. Both Ms. Marsden and the baby (35) are in good condition.

A spokesperson from East Texas Power said that unusually heavy use of air conditioners during the day probably caused (40) the blackout. "We've had two weeks of extremely hot weather, and everyone's had their air conditioners on full blast all that time. The plant just couldn't (45) take it," she admitted.

2   Comprehension. Answer the questions.

1. When did the blackout happen?
2. What did East Texas Power Company do when the electricity went off?
3. What did the police chief do? Why?
4. What happened at the baseball game?
5. What happened at the Conroy Building?
6. What caused the blackout?

3   Vocabulary building.

1. Sometimes you can figure out what a new word means from the way it is used in the sentence:
   He was cut by the broken glass when he *smashed* the window.
   What is the meaning of *smash*? How did you figure it out?

2. Sometimes a word looks like one you already know:
   Only a *handful* of people came to the party.
   What two words does *handful* contain? What do you think it means?

3. Many times you can only get an approximate meaning, but it is enough to continue reading:
   He bought a *modem* so he could send messages through his computer.

4. Sometimes you cannot figure out the meaning of the word, and it is necessary to the sentence. Then you have to look it up in the dictionary:
   Everyone agrees that the boy is a *genius*.
   Does this sentence make sense, if you don't know the word *genius*?

Now look at your list. Find the words you didn't know in the article.

1. Which new words did you figure out from the way they were used in the article?
2. Which ones did you have to look up in the dictionary?

Writing

Skill: Putting events in order
Task: Writing a story

1 When you tell a story, it is important to use time markers. They help the reader understand the order of the events of the story. Two of the time markers in the newspaper article on p. 26 are *when* and *after*. What others can you find?

2 Read these events from a story and rewrite them as a paragraph. Use the time markers in parentheses to connect them.

Note: You can write these sentences two ways:

When As soon as After	she finished, she left. OR She left	when as soon as after	she finished.

Note the comma.

1. A man went into the First National Bank.

(while)

2. He was standing in line.
3. A security guard noticed that he seemed nervous.

(when)

4. The man got to the teller's window.
5. He gave the teller a note.

(as soon as)

6. The security guard saw the teller give him a lot of money.
7. The security guard pulled the alarm.

(when)

8. The man tried to leave the bank.
9. The guard tried to stop him.

(as)

10. The man and the guard were fighting.
11. The guard's gun went off and the man was hit.

3 Now write a story about something unusual that happened to you. Before you write, organize the events of the story. Use time markers to make the order of the events clear.

For pronunciation exercises for Unit 3, see page 113.

A Heat Wave

1 Houston is having a heat wave. Cathy Wilson and her family are trying to decide what to do on Sunday. Listen to their conversation.

1

CATHY: You've been watching TV for two hours, Johnny. Why don't you go out and play?

JOHNNY: It's too hot to play outside. I want to go to a movie.

CATHY: We can't do that. Your sister isn't old enough. She'll annoy everyone.

2

KEN: What's the matter with Johnny?

CATHY: Nothing, really. He's just bored. Are there any jobs in the paper?

KEN: No. I'm really discouraged. I've been looking for work for three months.

CATHY: Don't worry, Ken. You're a good welder. There'll be an opening soon.

3

KEN: Why don't we go out today, Cathy? I'm too depressed to stay home.

CATHY: OK. But we can't go anywhere expensive. Remember our budget, Ken.

KEN: How about the Johnson Space Center? It's interesting, inexpensive and air conditioned.

CATHY: OK. I hope Johnny thinks it's as exciting as TV. Oh, I forgot. I've got to go to the mall to return that dress I bought.

KEN: That's OK. We can stop on the way.

2 Say *That's right, That's wrong* or *I don't know.*

1. Johnny wants to go outside.
2. Ken's looking for a job.
3. Cathy's worried about money.
4. Johnny likes spaceships.
5. They're going to stop at the store after they go to the space center.

3 Find a word or phrase in the conversation that means:

1. very unhappy
2. bother someone
3. take back
4. a plan of how to spend your money

4 Warm Up

Suggest a plan for the weekend.

A: Let's do something this weekend.

B: OK. *Let's go to the zoo.*

A: No, *it's too cold. Let's go bowling* instead.

OR Yes, that sounds *good. I love the elephants.*

DEVELOP YOUR VOCABULARY

How about *the beach?*	We could . . .
Why don't we . . . ?	. . .

Practice

A.

How long **has** Richie **been watching** TV?	He**'s been watching** TV	for two hours. since 9:00.
What **have** you **been doing** these days?	I**'ve been working** hard.	

1 Talk about the pictures.

1. A: How long has Richie been watching TV?
   B: He's been watching TV for two hours.

1. Richie / two hours

2. Juanita / lunchtime

3. Liz / one hour

4. Roger and Lois / a long time

5. Ann and Betty / 2:00

2 Ask a classmate what he or she has been doing recently.

A: What have you been doing *these days?*
B: I've been *learning how to drive.*

3 Ask classmates what they've been doing to improve their English.

A: What have you been doing to improve your English?
B: I've been *watching TV.*

DEVELOP YOUR VOCABULARY

since *you enrolled in this class* for *the last month*	lately recently

Student B can use these ideas:

read the newspaper	keep a journal
talk to neighbors	go to movies

> Ken **has been looking** for a job for three months.*
> He **has had** two interviews with Getty.**

*He's still looking. He's not finished yet.
**The two interviews are finished.

4 Linda and Pete are talking. Read the statements below. Then listen to their conversation and say if the statements are right or wrong.

1. Officer Brady just called Linda.
2. Officer Brady already spoke to Bill.
3. Linda doesn't know what Bill told Officer Brady.
4. Linda has talked to Bill.
5. The doctors are examining Bill.
6. Linda wants Pete to help her with the story.

5 Choose the sentence that describes the picture.

1. a. "But you've eaten your dinner."
   b. "But you've been eating your dinner."

2. a. "You've eaten the cake."
   b. "You've been eating the cake."

3. a. "I've ironed your blouse."
   b. "I've been ironing your blouse."

4. a. "I've read a book."
   b. "I've been reading a book."

6 Ken is talking to his brother Steve about looking for work. Read their conversation and complete it with the present perfect tense or the present perfect progressive tense of the verbs. Use the present perfect progressive when you can.

STEVE: How long have you _been looking_ for work now?
         1. look

KEN: Almost three months.

STEVE: Have you _____ the ads in the paper?
                      2. read

KEN: Oh, yes, I've _____ at least 50 ads by now. I think I've _____ to
                      3. answer   4. be
       every employment agency in town.

STEVE: Sometimes it just takes time, but I know it's difficult when you have nothing to do.

KEN: Yeah. I try to keep busy. I've already _____ the first floor, and I've
                                                5. paint
       _____ our bedroom. I'm almost finished.
          6. wallpaper

STEVE: Say, Ken, how about working as a security guard? I've _____ it for six
                                                                 7. do
       months now and it's not so bad.

KEN: I've _____ unemployed so long, I'll take any job.
             8. be

30

7 Talk about your work experience in this country.

A: How long have you been living *in the United States?*
B: *Two years.*
A: How many *jobs have you had so far?*
B: I've had *three.*
   OR   None. I haven't started working yet.

Now continue the conversation.
You can talk about these things:

write a résumé	get a promotion
go on job interviews	take a vacation

B.

Ellen's **too young** to go to the movies. She's **not old enough** to go.
Johnny's **old enough** to go. He's **not too young.**

1 Talk about the pictures. Use *too* or *enough.*

1. Johnny's old enough to see *Superman.*

1. old

2. young

3. small

4. big

5. short

6. tall

2 Talk about the people in the story. Use the adjectives in the box and *(not) enough* or *too.*

1. Bill Thomas can't leave the hospital yet.

A: Why can't Bill leave the hospital?

B: He's too weak.

2. Angela doesn't want Brad Kimball to interview the fire commissioner. She wants Linda to do it.
3. Pete Gómez wants to find a new apartment.
4. Tom Kirby isn't going to retire yet.
5. Michael Gómez will probably join the swimming team.
6. Linda doesn't go to the movies very often.

busy	old
experienced	small
good	~~weak~~

3 Ask a classmate about his or her abilities.

A: Do you think you could be *a newspaper reporter?*

B: Yes. I think so. I'm *aggressive enough to interview people.*

OR   No, I don't think so. I'm *too shy to talk to strangers.*

You can use these ideas:

dancer . . . graceful / clumsy
firefighter . . . strong / weak
basketball player . . . tall / short
soldier . . . old / young
secretary . . . efficient / disorganized

4 Bill Thomas is trying to identify the man who asked him to start the fires. Officer Brady is showing him three police sketches. Listen to the conversation and choose the correct sketch. Then talk about it with a classmate like this:

A: I think it's sketch . . .

B: I agree. It can't be sketch . . . His hair's not . . . enough.

OR   It can't be sketch . . . His hair's too . . .

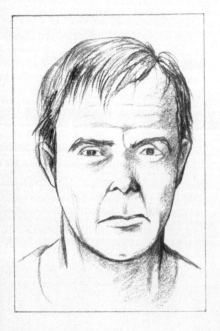

a   b   c

C.

Dallas isn't **as hot as** Houston.
It's **as rainy as** Houston.

1 **Everyone is talking about the weather. Look at the weather map and talk about the weather in these cities. Use the words in parentheses.**

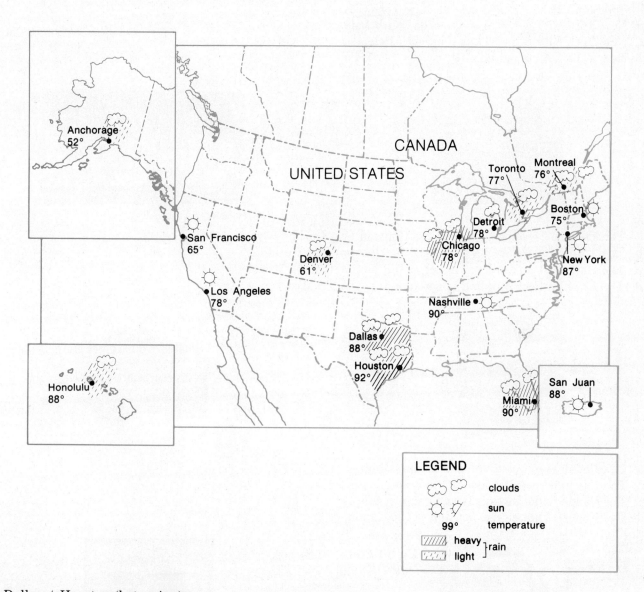

LEGEND

clouds

sun

99° temperature

heavy ⎤ rain
light ⎦

1. Dallas / Houston (hot, rainy)

A: Dallas isn't as hot as Houston.
B: Yes, but it's as rainy as Houston.

2. Honolulu / San Juan (hot, sunny)
3. Toronto / Montreal (cloudy, rainy)
4. San Francisco / Los Angeles (warm, sunny)
5. Miami / Nashville (hot, dry)
6. Detroit / Chicago (cloudy, warm)
7. Denver / Anchorage (cool, cloudy)
8. Boston / New York (hot, sunny)

2 Look at the pairs of photographs. Then read the sentences and decide which one is true.

New York City

The South Pole

1. a. The South Pole is not as cold as New York City.
   b. New York City is not as cold as the South Pole.
   c. New York City is as cold as the South Pole.
   d. New York City is not as warm as the South Pole.

Transco Tower

Houston Post Building

2. a. The Transco Tower is as tall as the Houston Post Building.
   b. The Transco Tower is not as tall as the Houston Post Building.
   c. The Houston Post Building is not as tall as the Transco Tower.
   d. The Houston Post Building is not as low as the Transco Tower.

Kodak

Canon

3. a. The Kodak is not as expensive as the Canon.
   b. The Canon is as expensive as the Kodak.
   c. The Canon is not as expensive as the Kodak.
   d. The Kodak is not as inexpensive as the Canon.

Margot

Carine

4. a. Margot is not as young as Carine.
   b. Carine is not as young as Margot.
   c. Margot is not as old as Carine.
   d. Margot is as old as Carine.

3   Compare the city or town you come from and the place you are living now.

A: Tell me about *Mexico City*. How does it compare
   to *Chicago?*

B: Well, *Mexico City* isn't as *modern* as *Chicago*, but
   it's *more exciting*.

DEVELOP YOUR VOCABULARY

crowded	muggy
polluted	picturesque
hectic	cosmopolitan
peaceful	scenic
huge	. . .

Just for Fun

**4   *Scrambled similes*. An expression which compares two things using *as . . . as* is
called a simile. Can you match the words with the pictures to complete these famous
English similes?**

1. as quiet as _g_
2. as cool as ____
3. as hungry as ____
4. as red as ____
5. as neat as ____
6. as light as ____
7. as rich as ____

a. a king

b. a beet

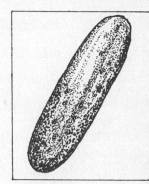
c. a cucumber

d. a feather

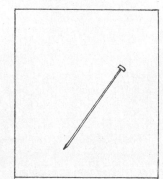
e. a pin

f. a lion

g. a mouse

Now make your own similes. Compare them to your classmates'.

1. As cold as _____
2. As depressed as _____
3. As old as _____
4. As hot as _____
5. As happy as _____

Life Skills

Shopping for clothes

For Your Information

Store refund policies

Refund policies are different from store to store, so it is important to check each store's policy before you buy something. At some stores there are no *refunds* or *exchanges*. Some stores only allow exchanges. Other stores only give you *store credit*. This means you have to buy something else at the same store for the same amount as your first item.

---

1 Cathy is at Peers Department Store. She is talking to a salesperson. Listen and complete their conversation.

CATHY: I'd like to ——————— this ———————.
                    1   2

SALESPERSON: What seems to be the ——————— with it?
                                              3

CATHY: Well, I usually ——————— a size ———————, but this is ———————
                                    4   5   6
              ——————— on me.
                  7

SALESPERSON: Would you like to ——————— it for a larger ———————?
                                          8   9

CATHY: No, I'd ——————— to get a ———————. I bought it only ——————— days
                        10   11   12
              ago.

SALESPERSON: Do you have your receipt?

CATHY: Yes, here it is.

SALESPERSON: OK. We'll be glad to give you your ——————— ———————.
                                                       13   14

**2 Roleplay a similar situation. You are in a department store.
    You want to return one of the items below.
    Student A is the customer.
    Student B is the salesperson.**

1. broken zipper

2. ?

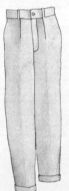

3. hole

4. wrong size

5. one leg longer than the other

6. stain

3 Another customer at Peers is trying to buy a pair of shoes. Read the conversation the customer is having with a salesperson.

CUSTOMER: I'd like to try on *these shoes*, but I'm not sure of my size in this country.
SALESPERSON: What size do you take in your country?
CUSTOMER: In *Italy* I take a size *44*.
SALESPERSON: Well, according to this chart, you take size *11* here.

Roleplay a similar conversation with a classmate. Use the information in the chart to talk about other items of clothing.

Clothing Sizes						
Women's						
suits, coats, jackets, dresses, blouses and sweaters						
U.S.	6	8	10	12	14	
Metric	36	38	40	42	44	
shoes						
U.S.	5	6	7	8	9	
Metric	35	36	37	38	39	

Men's							
suits, coats, jackets							
U.S.	34	36	38	40	42	44	46
Metric	44	46	48	50	52	54	56
shirts							
U.S.	14	14½	15	15½	16	16½	17
Metric	36	37	38	39	41	42	43
shoes							
U.S.	7	8	9	10	11	12	
Metric	40	41	42	43	44	45	

4 Cathy Wilson has a credit card at Peers. This is part of her last bill. Look at it and then read the statements below. Decide if the statements are right or wrong. If they are wrong, correct them.

ACCOUNT NUMBER	CLOSING DATE	DUE DATE				
214 255605 149	6/4/90	6/29/90	BILL INQUIRY NO. 736-5151			
STORE AND REFERENCE NO.	CHARGES	PAYMENTS & CREDITS	DEPT. NO.	DESCRIPTION		DATE
01 32484-2102	25.11		4193	MEN'S SPORTSWEAR		5-27
01 32484-2602	12.35		2106	CHILDREN'S		5-27
01 32864-698	63.00		4388	WOMEN'S		5-27
01 32484-231	15.29		2106	CHILDREN'S		5-31

PREVIOUS BALANCE	TOTAL CHARGES	TOTAL PAYMENTS AND CREDITS	AVERAGE DAILY BALANCE	FINANCE CHARGE	NEW BALANCE	MINIMUM PAYMENT (INCLUDES PAST DUE)
.00	115.75	.00	.00	.00	115.75	14.06

PEERS Department Store

	PERIODIC RATE	APPLIED TO THE FOLLOWING PORTION OF AVERAGE DAILY BALANCE	ANNUAL PERCENTAGE RATE
	%		%
	%		%
	1.65 %	0.00	19.8 %

1. Cathy bought three items.
2. Cathy bought two items in the same department.
3. Cathy has to pay this bill before June 4, 1990.
4. The bill is for $115.75.
5. Cathy has to pay the balance at one time.
6. If Cathy doesn't pay the new balance at one time, she will have to pay a finance charge next month.
7. Cathy has to pay a finance charge this month.

ON YOUR OWN
Think about Ken's problems and discuss these questions with your classmates.

1 What are some good ways of looking for a job?
2 Is there a high unemployment rate in your country? Can unemployed people receive financial help from your government? If so, how long can they receive it?

For pronunciation exercises for Unit 4, see page 113.

REVIEW 2

1 This is part of a letter that Cathy wrote to her sister. Complete the paragraph with the simple past or the past progressive form of the verbs.

Yesterday I _was working_ in the kitchen when a terrible thing _____ . I
             1. work   2. happen

_____ the dishes when I _____ a crash outside. I _____ to the window, and
3. wash   4. hear   5. go

I _____ a young boy. His motorcycle was lying on the ground, and he _____ to get
6. see   7. try

up. As soon as I _____ him, I _____ outside to see if I could help. He _____
8. see   9. run   10. sit

in the street. His arm _____ , but he _____ too badly hurt. I _____ to call
11. bleed   12. seem—neg.   13. go

an ambulance, when Dr. Nelson _____ by and _____ his car. He _____ the
14. drive   15. stop   16. take

boy to the hospital.

2 Make statements about what people *used to* do or *didn't use to* do 100 years ago.

1. travel by horse

They used to travel by horse.

2. have electric lights
3. wear long dresses all the time

4. use washing machines
5. wear contact lenses
6. cook all their meals over a fire
7. make telephone calls
8. live shorter lives

3 Complete this article with the correct form of the verbs. Use *used to* when you can.

The Houston Herald

Cooper Makes Big Mistake

Ed Cooper, head coach of the Houston Cavaliers, _used to be_ one of the best baseball coaches in the
        1. be

league. In fact, in 1987, he _____ "Coach of the Year." He
        2. win

understood the game better than anyone I've ever met, and

he _____ the confidence of his team. But that has changed.
  3. have

    Last night Ed Cooper _____ the biggest mistake
                  4. make

of his coaching career. He _____ star hitter, Mike Daniels.
        5. fire

Daniels, who _____ for the University of Houston, is very
       6. play

popular with the Houston fans. In addition, Daniels's

teammates _____ him "Most Valuable Player" last year.
      7. name

Why _____ Cooper _____ this excellent player?
            8. fire

Because Daniels _____ practice one day. Although it's
         9. miss

important that players on a baseball team practice, perhaps

Cooper should give Daniels another chance.

4 Match the phrases in columns A and B. Then combine the phrases with *to*.

A		B
1. _d._	Officer Brady told Linda	a. use a computer
2. ____	Pete would like Tom	b. meet him at a factory
3. ____	Pete encourages Michael	c. take some pictures
4. ____	Cathy wants Minh	d. be careful
5. ____	Bill asked Linda	e. study hard
6. ____	Angela reminded Brad	f. get the information to Linda

1. Officer Brady told Linda to be careful.

5 **What has Ken been doing since he lost his job? Write about his activities. Use the present perfect progressive tense.**

1. work around the house

He's been working around the house.

2. do the cooking
3. go to the grocery store

4. answer ads
5. take care of the children
6. drive Cathy to work
7. visit employment agencies

6 **Look at the time line of Ken's life. Then read the answers and write questions in the present perfect progressive or present perfect tense. Begin the questions with** *How long.*

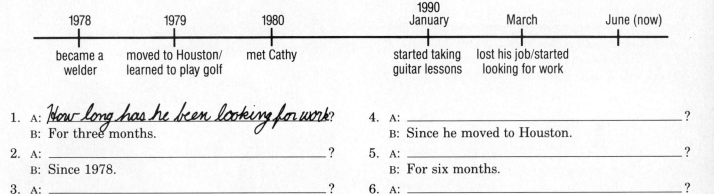

1978	1979	1980	1990 January	March	June (now)
became a welder	moved to Houston/ learned to play golf	met Cathy	started taking guitar lessons	lost his job/started looking for work	

1. A: *How long has he been looking for work?*
   B: For three months.
2. A: _____ ?
   B: Since 1978.
3. A: _____ ?
   B: Since 1979.
4. A: _____ ?
   B: Since he moved to Houston.
5. A: _____ ?
   B: For six months.
6. A: _____ ?
   B: Since 1980.

7 **Complete these sentences with the adjectives and** *(not) enough* **or** *too.*

1. Tom Kirby is only 60. He's *not old enough*
   _{old}
   to retire.
2. Ellen Wilson is _____ to go to school.
   _{young}
3. Don't worry about Linda. She's _____ to take
   _{old}
   care of herself.
4. Tom is very smart. In fact, he was _____ to go
   _{smart}
   to college at the age of 15.

5. Ken doesn't feel like going to the party.
   He's _____ .
   _{depressed}
6. Michael doesn't have to go to the doctor.
   He's _____ .
   _{sick}
7. Brad can't be a basketball player. He's _____ .
   _{short}
8. Ken's _____ to be an actor.
   _{shy}

8 **Look at the information about California and Texas. Make comparisons using** *not as . . . as* **with the adjectives in parentheses.**

	California	*Texas*
year founded	1769	1682
area	158,693 sq. mi.	267,338 sq. mi.
population density	168.6 people per sq. mi.	62.5 people per sq. mi.
per capita income	$15,255	$13,165
average annual rainfall	14.85" (Los Angeles)	44.76" (Houston)

Information as of 1985

1. *California isn't as old as Texas.* (old)
2. _____ (large)
3. _____ (crowded)
4. _____ (wealthy*)

Now Compare Los Angeles and Houston.

5. _____ (dry)

*wealthy = rich

Two Heads Are Better Than One

1 Linda and Pete are working late at the office. Listen to their conversation.

1

PETE: You've been working too hard, Linda. Why don't you take a break and get a bite to eat with me?

LINDA: I can't eat. I'm too discouraged. I'm not getting anywhere with this arson story.

PETE: This type of work *can* be discouraging. Why don't you tell me about it? You know what they say—two heads are better than one.

LINDA: OK. Maybe you'll be able to help.

2

PETE: So, what's going on?

LINDA: Well, Bill told the police that a man asked him to start those fires but he refused.

PETE: That's interesting. Did he know the guy?

LINDA: No, but he was able to describe him. Here's a copy of the artist's sketch.

3

PETE: I hope the police will be able to find him soon. He looks mean. You should be very careful, Linda.

LINDA: Don't worry. I can take care of myself.

2 Give a reason for these facts.

1. Pete wants Linda to take a break.
2. Linda feels discouraged.
3. The police artist was able to make a sketch of the man who asked Bill to start the fires.
4. Pete is worried about Linda.

3 Find a word or phrase in the conversation that means:

1. said no
2. could describe
3. not making progress
4. unkind

4 Warm Up

Ask a classmate if he or she can help you with something.

A: Can you help me with *my homework* later?

B: Sure. I'll be able to help you *tonight*.

OR Sorry. I won't be able to help you. *I have to go to the dentist.*

DEVELOP YOUR VOCABULARY

income taxes	application form
report	term paper
. . .	. . .

Practice

A.

> Linda is **discouraged** about her work.
> Sometimes her work is **discouraging.**

1 Use the adjectives to describe the pictures.

1. Linda's discouraged.
   Her work is discouraging.

1. discouraged / discouraging

2. bored / boring

3. annoyed / annoying

4. excited / exciting

5. interested / interesting

2 Linda and Cathy are talking. Read their conversation and complete it with an adjective ending in -ed or -ing.

LINDA: What's wrong, Cathy?

CATHY: Oh, it's Ken. You know he's been looking for work for three months and he's getting

really _____ . I try to be _____ to him, but even I'm getting _____ .
1. discourage   2. encourage   3. depress

LINDA: I'm sorry. I know that looking for a job can be _____ . Believe me, I was
4. depress

_____ when I got this job.
5. please

3 Listen to the conversations. Then describe these people with an adjective from the box.

1. Johnny is _____ .
2. Ellen is _____ .
3. The woman is _____ .
4. Johnny is _____ .
5. Cathy is _____ .

annoyed	annoying
discouraged	discouraging
frightened	frightening
~~excited~~	exciting
tired	tiring

4 Talk about your English language experience.

1. What was your most embarrassing moment in trying to speak English?
2. What kinds of classroom language activities do you think are interesting?
3. What kinds of activities do you think are boring?
4. What is the most confusing thing about English?

B.

He	**was(n't) able to** find a job last month.
	has(n't) been able to find a job yet.
	will (won't) be able to find a job soon.

1 Can you remember the story? Make sentences with *has/have been able to* or *was/were able to*.

1. Ken / find a job yet

Ken hasn't been able to find a job yet.

2. Bill / identify the driver of the car after the accident
3. The police / catch the arsonist yet
4. The firefighters / put out the fire before it destroyed the factory

5. Cathy and her family / go to the Johnson Space Center last weekend
6. Pete / find a job in Houston two months after he moved there
7. Angela / ski since her accident
8. Michael / finish his homework during the blackout

2 Each person in the pictures has a problem. Make a suggestion to help him or her. Use *will be able to.*

1. A: She can't do the crossword puzzle.
   B: Why doesn't she use the dictionary? Then she'll be able to do it.

1. She can't do the crossword puzzle.

2. She can't skate.

3. He can't do his taxes.

4. She can't read the letter.

5. He can't put the bicycle together.

3 Linda is calling the Houston *Herald*. Listen to the conversation and choose the correct message form.

PHONE MESSAGE
to: *Pete Gómez*
from: *Linda Smith*
She won't be able to meet you. Please call her at home.

1

PHONE MESSAGE
to: *Pete Gómez*
from: *Linda Smith*
She would like to meet with you this morning after she speaks to Officer Brady.

2

PHONE MESSAGE
to: *Pete Gómez*
from: *Linda Smith*
She won't be able to meet you. She's gone to see Officer Brady.

3

4 Talk about what you hope you'll be able to do in the future.

A: I hope I'll be able to *speak English really well in three years.*

B: I hope I'll be able to *have my own business.*

You can use these ideas:

buy *a house*
get a job as *a bilingual secretary*
move to *Dallas*
open *a beauty salon*

C.

I You He She We You They	can take care of	myself. yourself. himself. herself. ourselves. yourselves. themselves.

1 Describe what the people or animals are doing in the pictures.

1. Pete's looking at himself.

1. look at

Now this goes here . . .

2. talk to

3. scratch

4. dress

Cathy takes care of Ken, and Ken takes care of Cathy.
They take care of **each other.**

5. write

6. stare at

7. chase

2 Pete is having lunch with Linda. Complete the conversation with a *-self/-selves* pronoun or *each other*.

PETE: Have you spoken to Bill again?

LINDA: Yes. We spoke to *each other* ___ yesterday. He's really upset with
    1

_____ because of his past. Now he says everyone thinks he's the arsonist.
    2

PETE: Do you think he's gotten _____ into trouble again?
    3

LINDA: No. But I *do* think he's in danger. I'm not sure that Bill and his mother can

take care of _____. I think they need police protection.
    4

PETE: And what about *you?* Can you take care of _____?
    5

LINDA: Oh, I'm not worried about _____.
    6

(Tom enters restaurant)

TOM: You two don't look like you're enjoying _____ very much.
    7

PETE: It's this arson case. Linda is driving _____ crazy over it.
    8

TOM: Maybe we should all go out to a movie after work and try to enjoy _____
    9

for a change.

3 Ask what someone did last weekend.

A: What did *your children* do last weekend?
B: *They went bowling.*
A: Did *they* enjoy *themselves?*
B: Yes, *they* did.
    OR   No, *they* didn't. *The place was too crowded.*

Just for Fun

4 Read Dr. Cousins's column from the *Herald* and follow the instructions.

Dear Dr. Cousins

Do You Like Yourself?

Take this short test and see for yourself.

YES NO

1. Do you enjoy yourself when you are alone? ☐ ☐

2. Do you always talk about yourself when you are with other people? ☐ ☐

3. Do you say nice things about yourself? ☐ ☐

4. Do you look at yourself a lot in the mirror? ☐ ☐

5. Do you often feel sorry for yourself? ☐ ☐

YES NO

6. Do you get angry with yourself when you make a mistake? ☐ ☐

7. Do you usually feel good about yourself when you meet new people? ☐ ☐

Scoring: Give yourself 1 point for a *yes* answer in questions 1, 3 and 7. Give yourself 1 point for a *no* answer in questions 2, 4, 5 and 6. The more points you have, the more you like yourself.

PUT IT ALL TOGETHER
Cathy and Ken are talking about his problem. Listen and complete their conversation.

CATHY: You look so _____ 1 , Ken. You're driving _____ 2 crazy.

KEN: I know, but I can't stop _____ 3 from thinking about work.

CATHY: Don't be so _____ 4 . I'm sure _____ 5 _____ 6 _____ 7 _____ 8
find something soon.

KEN: I know. I tell _____ 9 that every day, but nothing happens. It's really very

_____ 10 . Two years ago I _____ 11 _____ 12 _____ 13 get a job
without any problem.

CATHY: But times are a lot harder now, Ken.

KEN: You're right, Cath. I should stop worrying.

CATHY: Let's go to a movie. We need to enjoy _____ 14 a little. We can ask your brother to

_____ 15 _____ 16 _____ 17 the kids. I think we need some time alone with

_____ 18 _____ 19 .

Now roleplay a similar situation.
Student A has a problem that has no easy solution.
**Student B offers encouragement and suggests an activity to take Student A's mind
off the problem.**

Student A can use these ideas:

> You've been looking for an apartment and haven't
> been able to find one.
> You are overworked at your job.
> You broke your arm and will have to wear a cast
> for six weeks.
> You've been trying to learn how to use a computer
> and feel frustrated.

ON YOUR OWN
Discuss these questions with your classmates.

1 Think of a problem you recently had. What did
you do to try to solve it? Do you believe "two
heads are better than one," or do you usually
prefer to solve problems by yourself?

2 Sometimes people with problems get help from
professionals (job counselors, academic advisers,
psychologists, clergy, social workers). Are these
professionals common in your country?

Reading

1 **Skimming. Sometimes you read an article quickly to find out what it's about. Read this article as quickly as you can. Then choose the best headline from the list below. Discuss why you chose the headline.**

1. TEXAS OILMAN GIVES MUSEUM $1 MILLION
2. HOUSTON ART MUSEUM TO OPEN RESTAURANT
3. THE NEW HOUSTON ART MUSEUM: A PLACE FOR ALL
4. AN ART MUSEUM FOR CHILDREN

The Houston Herald

An art museum is usually quiet and peaceful. People generally speak quietly, if they speak at all. The Houston Art (5) Museum, however, isn't as quiet as it used to be. When I visited it two days ago, I saw a very different scene. Instead of art lovers whispering quietly, it was (10) full of workers carrying lumber, bricks and tools. The sound of hammering and sawing combined with shouting made it the noisiest art museum I've ever (15) visited. But don't worry, this is not a new idea in art. The Houston Art Museum is simply undergoing a major renovation.

According to museum (20) director Frank Jordan, there were several reasons for the renovation. First of all, the museum was no longer big enough to hold all the paintings. (25) "We have acquired more than 150 new paintings in the past two years, and we just didn't have room for them," he said. Another reason for the (30) renovation was to add a restaurant and a children's art room. Jordan explained, "We decided to add the restaurant because we wanted to make the (35) art museum more a part of people's lives. We're hoping that people will start saying, 'Let's meet for lunch at the art museum.'" The children's room (40) is a project that is close to Jordan's heart. "We also wanted the art museum to be a place for families, so we decided to create a 'children's room.' We'll (45) use it as a place to display art by children as well as a place for children to learn how to create art. We're one of the first art museums in the country (50) to do this."

And how are they paying for this expensive project? According to Jordan, Texas oilman and art lover Evans (55) Collier gave the museum one million dollars for the renovation. In order to thank him, Jordan says that the new section of the museum will be (60) called the Evans Collier Wing.

When the museum renovation is complete next fall, the museum won't be as small as it was, and with the addition of (65) the children's room it probably won't be as quiet either. However, if Jordan and the museum directors are right, it will truly be a place for all.

---

2 **Comprehension. Reread the article and answer these questions.**

1. What is happening at the Houston Art Museum?
2. Why did they decide to make the museum larger? (Give three reasons.)
3. What are they going to name the new section of the museum? Why?

3 **Finding the main idea. The main idea of the first paragraph is found in the last sentence (lines 16, 17 and 18):**

The Houston Art Museum is simply undergoing a major renovation.

Find the sentences that give the main idea of paragraphs 2, 3 and 4.

Writing

Skill: Stating reasons
Task: Writing a paragraph explaining a decision

1 **When we give reasons for things we do, we often use the words *because, so* and *therefore.***

a. *Because* states a reason:

> **Result**   **Reason**
> We stopped for lunch **because** we were hungry.

Notice there is no comma before *because*.

b. *So* and *therefore* state results:

> **Reason**   **Result**
> We were hungry, **so** we stopped for lunch.

Notice there is a comma before *so*.

> **Reason**   **Result**
> We were hungry; **therefore,** we stopped for lunch.
> OR   We were hungry. **Therefore,** we stopped for lunch.

Notice there is a semicolon before *therefore*. Also
notice *therefore* can begin a new sentence.

2 **Connect each sentence two ways with the words in parentheses.**

1. I came to the United States. I wanted a better job. (because) (so)
I came to the United States because I wanted a better job.
I wanted a better job, so I came to the United States.
2. I hated working in the factory. I quit my job. (because) (therefore)
3. My father lost his job at home. He decided to come to the United States. (therefore) (because)
4. My parents don't feel comfortable here. They plan to return home. (so) (because)
5. I wanted my children to have more opportunities than I had. My wife and I decided to move here. (so) (because)
6. There weren't many opportunities in my hometown. I moved to the capital. (because) (therefore)

3 **Make a list of the reasons for making an important decision in your life. Some important decisions might include why you:**

1. moved to a different city or country.
2. decided to study English.
3. decided (not) to take a certain job.

4 **Use your list of reasons to write a paragraph about why you made the important decision. Try to use *because, so* and *therefore*.**

For pronunciation exercises for Unit 5, see page 113.

A Special Delivery Letter

1 Brad is looking for Linda. He has something to give her. Listen to the conversation.

1

BRAD: Pete, have you seen Linda? A special delivery letter just came for her.

PETE: No. But if I see her, I'll tell her.

BRAD: Thanks. By the way, are you enjoying working in Houston?

PETE: Yes. But I miss Dallas sometimes.

2

LINDA: Hi, guys. I just finished talking to Bill. What's happening here?

BRAD: This just came for you.

LINDA: I don't believe it! It's a threatening letter!

BRAD: What? Who sent it? What's it about?

LINDA: I don't know who sent it. It's anonymous. But it's about my arson stories.

PETE: I kept warning you this could be dangerous.

BRAD: You'd better call the police.

PETE: Yes. This is serious. If *you* don't call, *I* will!

3

LINDA: Can I speak to Officer Brady, please?

CLERK: Sorry, but he's not here now. Can I take a message?

LINDA: Yes. Please tell him that Linda Smith from the *Herald* called. I have to speak to him immediately. It's urgent!

2 Say *That's right, That's wrong* or *I don't know.*

1. Linda received a letter.
2. Pete doesn't like working in Houston.
3. Pete misses working at the Dallas *Star.*
4. Linda knows who sent the letter.
5. Linda spoke to Officer Brady on the phone.

3 Find a word or phrase in the conversation that means:

1. without a name
2. you should
3. very important
4. continued

4 Warm Up

Tell a classmate about something you miss.

A: I really miss *my hometown.*

B: I know what you mean. I miss *my friends.*

You can use these ideas:

types of food	certain places
holiday celebrations	possessions

Practice

A.

> **If** Pete **finds** a bigger apartment, he**'ll move**.
> **If** he **doesn't find** one, he **won't move**.

1 What will happen if . . .? Match the possible events in column A with their correct results in column B. Give a reason for your choices like this:

1. If Pete finds a bigger apartment, he'll move because he needs more room.

A		B	
1.	<u>d.</u> If Pete finds a bigger apartment, he	a.	will get sick.
2.	____ If Ken finds a job, he	b.	will move to Houston.
3.	____ If Michael doesn't study hard, he	c.	will celebrate.
4.	____ If the police don't catch the hit-and-run driver, Bill	d.	will move.
5.	____ If Linda doesn't relax more, she	e.	won't feel safe.
6.	____ If the lights go out again, Tom	f.	won't pass his test.
7.	____ If Suzanne gets a job at the *Herald*, she	g.	won't lose the story he's working on.

2 Linda is talking to Cathy. Listen to their conversation and find out what Linda will do if she gets another threatening letter.

1. Stop working on the arson story.
2. Work harder on the arson story. ✔
3. Write about the letter in the newspaper.
4. Tell Alice Thomas.
5. Call Officer Brady.
6. Ask for police protection.
7. Go live with Cathy for a while.
8. Ask Angela for help.

3 Complete these sentences with information about yourself. Then tell a classmate.

1. If I study hard, . . .
2. If I don't speak English every day, . . .
3. I'll ask the teacher if . . .
4. I won't be happy if . . .

4 It's a busy day at the newsroom. Say what will or won't happen if . . .

If Tom doesn't close the window, the papers will fly out.

Just for Fun _____

⟨⟨⟨⟨⟨⟨⟨⟨THE CHAIN GAME⟩⟩⟩⟩⟩⟩⟩⟩

5 **One student says a sentence with *if* or *will*. The next student uses part of that sentence to say a new sentence. Continue around the class and see how many ideas you can think of. Look at the example and use your imagination.**

A: If I stay home, I'll get bored.
B: If I get bored, I'll call my friend.
C: If I call my friend, we'll talk for hours.

D: If we talk for hours, I'll get a big phone bill.
E: If I get a big phone bill, . . .

_____

B.

Linda's in danger.
Linda **had better** call Officer Brady.
She**'d better not** investigate the case anymore.

she'd better = she had better

Note: We don't use *had better* in affirmative questions.

1 **What are the people saying? Use *had better* or *had better not*.**

You'd better call the police.

1. call

2. study

3. hit

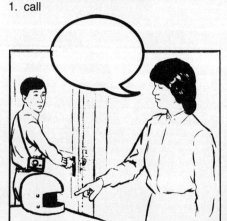

4. forget

5. come

2 Officer Brady is returning Linda's phone call. Listen to their conversation. Then choose the letter Linda received.

3 Officer Brady is at the *Herald* talking to Linda and Angela. Complete their conversation with *had better* or *had better not*.

BRADY: I think you*'d better not work* on this case anymore. You're making someone
1. work

nervous. And you _____ me everything you know.
2. tell

ANGELA: In fact, Linda, maybe you _____ leaving town for a while.
3. consider

LINDA: I can't just run away.

ANGELA: Well, you _____ with someone then. Why don't you come stay with me until this
4. stay

is cleared up?

BRADY: That's a good idea.

LINDA: OK. I'll go home and pack some things.

BRADY: Wait for me. I _____ you. Oh, and you _____ anyone else about this letter.
5. drive   6. tell

I _____ about it in the *Herald*.
7. read

ANGELA: Don't worry, Officer. I'll make sure that no one here says anything. In fact, I

_____ that now. And I think I _____ everyone that Linda has stopped
8. do   9. tell

investigating the case.

4 **Decide what the people should say in the situations.**

1. a. "Would you please obey the speed limit?"
   b. "You'd better obey the speed limit."
   c. "It's a good idea to obey the speed limit."

2. a. "You'd better buy me some ice cream."
   b. "You should buy me some ice cream."
   c. "Please buy me some ice cream."

3. a. "Could I have the day off?"
   b. "You'd better give me the day off."
   c. "You should give me the day off."

4. a. "You should see this movie."
   b. "You'd better see this movie."
   c. "Would you please see this movie?"

5 **Give a classmate advice about a health problem that you or someone you know has.**

A: What's the matter?
B: I'm worried about *my sister. She has a terrible rash.*
A: Hmm. That sounds serious. *She*'d better see *a dermatologist.*

DEVELOP YOUR VOCABULARY

internist	ulcer, kidney stones
orthopedist	sore *arm*, back problems
podiatrist	ingrown toenail, fallen arches
ophthalmologist	double vision, blurred vision
psychologist	anxiety, depression, insomnia
. . .	. . .

C.

> Pete enjoys **working** in Houston, but he misses **seeing** his girlfriend.

Some other verbs that are followed by the verb + -*ing* (the gerund):			
avoid	deny	keep	start
consider	dislike	practice	stop
continue	have trouble	remember	suggest

1 Can you remember the story? Ask questions with the phrases below. Then ask your classmates.

1. Who / enjoys / work in Houston
A: Who enjoys working in Houston?
B: Pete does.
2. Who denied / start the fires
3. Who's having trouble / find a job
4. Who enjoys / paint
5. Who dislikes / work on a computer
6. Who just started / study computer programming
7. Who misses / see his girlfriend
8. Who's avoided / ask for help
9. Who suggested / call the police

Bill   Angela   Pete

Tom   Linda   Brad   Ken

2 Linda is at Angela's apartment. Complete their conversation with the gerund.

LINDA: What beautiful paintings, Angela! Are they yours?

ANGELA: No, I enjoy _painting_ , but I'm not *that* good. These belong to the art museum.
            1. paint
            We're just keeping them until they finish _____ the renovation.
            2. do

LINDA: You're lucky to have them.

ANGELA: Well, yes and no. I don't even enjoy _____ out anymore. I'm too nervous about the
            3. go
            paintings.

LINDA: Do you have all the museum's paintings here?

ANGELA: Oh, no! We avoided _____ the most valuable ones here. They're in a warehouse
            4. bring
            downtown.

3 Talk about your likes and dislikes.

A: I really like cooking, but I don't like *doing the dishes.*
B: I like *reading*, but I don't like *looking up words in the dictionary.*

4 Talk about your childhood.

1. What did you enjoy doing when you were a child?
2. What did you dislike doing?
3. Was there anything you had trouble doing?
4. Was there anything you had to practice doing?

Life Skills

Telephone calls

🔲

1 Cathy Wilson received a phone call while she was away from her desk. Listen to the call and then complete the message. Use today's date and the correct time.

IMPORTANT MESSAGE

TO _____

DATE _____ TIME _____ A.M.
                                      P.M.

WHILE YOU WERE OUT

M _____

OF _____

Area Code
& Exchange _____

TELEPHONED		WILL CALL AGAIN	
CALLED TO SEE YOU		URGENT	
WANTS TO SEE YOU		RETURNED YOUR CALL	
PLEASE CALL			

Message _____

_____

_____

_____

🔲

2 Pete Gómez is calling directory assistance to ask for someone's phone number. Listen to the conversation and complete it.

OPERATOR: Hello. Mrs. Ketcham.

PETE: Hello. Can I have the _____ of John _____ ?
                              1   2

OPERATOR: Can you _____ the _____ _____ , please?
                     3   4   5

PETE: It's ____-____-____-____-____-____-____ .
                       6

OPERATOR: _____ as in _____ ?
              7   8

PETE: No, _____ as in _____ .
             9   10

OPERATOR: And do you know the _____ ?
                               11

PETE: Yes, _____ Grove Street.
              12

OPERATOR: The _____ is _____ .
                 13   14

PETE: _____ ?
         15

OPERATOR: Yes, that's right.

PETE: Thank you.

3 Now roleplay a similar situation.

Student A calls directory assistance and asks for the number of someone from the list on the left.

Student B is the operator and uses the information from the phone book. If Student B can't find the number, he or she will say, "There's no listing."

```
Jeff Groman, 1836 Wood

Ann Grometstein, 39 Kane Street

John Gromek, 3162 Lamar

Melinda Gromit, 29 Maple

Karl Gromis, 10713 Winkler

Edith Gromm, 1403 University Blvd

Arthur Grombach, 8210 Memorial Dr.

Robert Gromek, 115 West Main

Bob Gromet, 3816 Broadway

Maria Grondski, 2136 Hamilton
```

4 Pete is calling John Baretta. He is not there. Listen to John's answering machine and choose the message Pete left for him.

1. "Mr. Baretta, please call me back at 928–2413. Thank you."
2. "This is Pete Gómez. It's 5:00. Please call me at 6:00."
3. "This is Pete Gómez from the Houston *Herald* calling at 5:00 P.M. Please call me back at 928–2413."

5 Match the sentences in columns A and B to make short conversations.

A

1. Can I speak to Monica, please?

2. I'm sorry. I dialed the wrong number.

3. Can I leave a message?

4. At the sound of the beep, please leave a short message.

5. I'd like the number of Edward Ulin, please.

B

a. That's quite all right.

b. Speaking.

c. This is Vilma Ortiz at 928–1873. Please return my call before 5:00.

d. Could you spell the last name, please?

e. Sure. Please hold on while I get a pen.

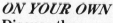
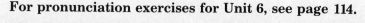

ON YOUR OWN
Discuss these questions with your classmates.

1 Do you prefer to talk to someone on the phone or in person? Why?

2 How do you feel about speaking English on the phone? Why?

3 Are telephone answering machines common in your country? If so, who has them? (businesses? homes?) How do you feel about leaving a message on one?

For pronunciation exercises for Unit 6, see page 114.

REVIEW 3

1   Michael is talking to Pete about his schoolwork. Complete their conversation with the -ed or -ing form of the words.

MICHAEL: Dad, I'm still _discouraged_ about
1. discourage

my bad grades. I'm really _____ of
2. tire

studying hard and not doing well.

PETE: What's the problem? Are your classes

_____ ?
3. bore

MICHAEL: No. They're very _____ , and I'm
4. interest

really _____ about my science
5. excite

project.

PETE: What does your teacher say?

MICHAEL: She's really _____ to me. She says I
6. encourage

shouldn't get _____ about things
7. depress

and that I should keep trying.

PETE: That's true. Starting a new school is often

hard, you know, and a little _____ .
8. frighten

It's nothing to feel _____ about.
9. embarrass

MICHAEL: I know, Dad. It's just that I never had

trouble before and I feel _____ . I
10. disappoint

really want to do well.

PETE: I know you're _____ , Michael. But
11. disappoint

I'm _____ with your attitude, and
12. please

I'm sure you'll do better soon.

2   Can you remember the story? Complete these sentences with the correct form of be able to.

1. Pete is very friendly. He _has been able to_ _____ make a lot of new friends since he moved to Houston.
2. Tom _____ go to the movies last night. He had too much work.
3. Suzanne _____ move to Houston if she gets a job.
4. The doctors _____ help Bill after he was hit by the car.
5. The police _____ catch the arsonist yet.
6. The firefighters tried, but they _____ put out the fire.
7. Pete hopes that he _____ find a bigger apartment.
8. A few years ago Ken _____ find a job without any problem.

3   Complete this chart.

1. myself   _____   I
2. _____   they
3. herself   _____
4. _____   he

5. _____   we
6. yourselves   _____
7. _____   you

4   Complete these questions with a reflexive pronoun or *each other*. Then answer them.

1. A: How do you enjoy _yourself_ ?
   B: _____ .

2. A: What do you and your friends talk to _____ about?
   B: _____ .

3. A: How often do you and your friends speak to _____ in English?
   B: _____ .

4. A: When you were a child, did you ever hurt _____ ? How?
   B: _____ .

5. A: Why's Michael Gómez disappointed with _____ ?
   B: _____ .

6. A: Do you think Linda can take care of _____ ?
   B: _____ .

56

5 Match the phrases in columns A and B. Then combine them with *if* and *will / won't*.

	A		**B**
1. *d.*	you don't study	a.	be late
2. ____	he works too hard	b.	make a lot of money
3. ____	she is successful	c.	gain weight
4. ____	I drive too fast	d.	not pass
5. ____	we don't leave soon	e.	get sick
6. ____	you don't exercise	f.	have an accident

1. If you don't study, you won't pass.

6 Read these situations. Then write what each person *had better* or *had better not* do.

1. Tom's flying to Los Angeles this morning. It's 10:00, and his plane leaves at 10:20. He isn't at the airport yet.

He'd better hurry.

2. Cathy has been feeling sick for the last few days.
3. Ken would like to buy a new car, but he knows that he doesn't have the money now.
4. Linda hasn't spoken to her parents for two months.
5. Bill would like to go back to work, but the doctor has told him not to.

7 Make sentences with these words.

1. Tom / enjoys / go to movies

Tom enjoys going to movies.

2. Ken / keeps / look for a job
3. Bill / denied / start the fires
4. Michael / has trouble / get good grades
5. Pete / misses / see Suzanne
6. The police / haven't stopped / look for the arsonist
7. Angela / suggested / take a break
8. Brad / practices / play tennis

8 Match the sentences in column A and B. Then combine them with *therefore*.

	A		**B**
1. *d*	Linda words too hard.	a.	The police suspected him of arson.
2. ____	Tom doesn't like computers.	b.	He feels discouraged.
3. ____	Angela had a bad accident.	c.	He uses a typewriter.
4. ____	Cathy writes restaurant reviews.	d.	She's always tired.
5. ____	Bill used to get into trouble.	e.	He calls her a lot.
6. ____	Pete misses Suzanne.	f.	She often eats out.
7. ____	Ken can't find a job.	g.	She walks with a cane.

1. Linda words too hard; therefore, she's always tired.

Now rewrite the sentences with *because*.

1. Because Linda works too hard, she's always tired.
   OR   Linda's always tired because she works too hard.

1 Linda, Angela, her husband Frank and Frank's assistant are having dinner at Angela's. Listen to their conversation.

1

CAROL: Being a newspaper reporter sounds so exciting, Linda. Writing about politics and investigating crimes is just so interesting. I want to hear all about your work.

LINDA: Well, most of it's done at my desk—like any office job. It's really just routine.

CAROL: Routine? Getting threatening letters isn't just routine.

2

ANGELA: What? How did you hear about that? Only a couple of people at the paper and the police know.

CAROL: Didn't someone here just mention it?

FRANK: *I* don't remember talking about threatening letters.

CAROL: Well, maybe I overheard it at the museum. I'm not sure now . . .

3

ANGELA: Linda, it's for you. It's Cathy.

CATHY: Guess what! Ken's brother Steve just got him a job! How about joining us for dinner tomorrow night? We feel like celebrating.

2 Say *That's right, That's wrong* or *I don't know.*

1. Linda and Carol are close friends.
2. Carol doesn't like her job.
3. Linda thinks her job is always exciting.
4. Frank told Carol about the letter.
5. Cathy and Ken are happy about his new job.

4 Warm Up

Talk about a job you'd like to have.

A: I'd like to be *a flight attendant*.
B: I wouldn't. It's too *tiring*.
  OR So would I. It's very *exciting*.

3 Find a word or phrase in the conversation that means:

1. heard accidentally
2. coming with us
3. say something about it

DEVELOP YOUR VOCABULARY

astronaut	hairdresser
bartender	paramedic
comedian	social worker
court reporter	. . .

Practice

A.

> **Reading** is Linda's favorite pastime.
>
> She's good **at writing** about crime and politics.
> She'll keep **on covering** the arson story.

1 Say what each person's favorite pastime is.

1. Reading is Linda's favorite pastime.

1. Linda

2. Minh

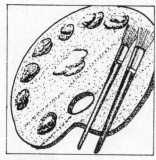

3. Angela

4. Pete

5. Tom

6. Cathy

2 Linda's having dinner with Ken and Cathy. Listen and complete their conversation.

LINDA: Are you excited about _starting_ your new job, Ken?
                               1

KEN: Well, I'm certainly looking forward to _____ again. I'm really tired of _____ home.
                                            2   3

CATHY: Ken's going to keep on _____ for a job as a welder. _____ a security guard is
                              4   5
just temporary.

LINDA: I understand. It's better to have a job at something you're good at _____.
                                                                          6

KEN: Yes, but I'm thankful to my brother for _____ me this job. It's great to be able to
                                             7
read the paper without _____ depressed.
                       8

CATHY: Talking about _____ depressed, Linda, how do you feel about _____ at
                     9   10
Angela's? You probably miss _____ at home.
                            11

LINDA: Oh, it's OK. Last night, her husband's assistant, Carol Fullerton, came over for dinner.

CATHY: How was that? Is she nice?

LINDA: A little strange. She was *very* interested in _____ all about the arson story.
                                                     12

3 Ask a classmate about his or her favorite pastime or sport.

A: What's your favorite *pastime?*
B: *Taking long walks.* What about you?
A: Oh, I always look forward to *playing cards with my friends.*

Just for Fun

4 Complete these horoscopes. Use a gerund (verb + *ing*) and any other words you need. Then tell a classmate his or her horoscope.

The Houston Herald

Your Horoscope

♈ Aries (March 21–April 19) Spend time *doing things* with a good friend. Avoid _____ at night. Don't worry about _____ .

♉ Taurus (April 20–May 20) Enjoy _____ alone. Don't think a lot about _____ , money is a bad idea.

♊ Gemini (May 21–June 20) Keep on _____ . You can look forward to _____ something interesting. _____ every day is a good idea.

♋ Cancer (June 21–July 22) Avoid _____ too much. You're good at _____ , so do more of that. _____ is a good idea.

♌ Leo (July 23–August 22) Don't be too interested in _____ with your family. You can enjoy _____ alone.

♍ Virgo (August 23–September 22) You'd better act now if you are interested in _____ . Start _____ before it's too late.

♎ Libra (September 23–October 22) Stop _____ to your friends. If you feel like _____ , that's fine.

♏ Scorpio (October 23–November 21) Worry more about _____ every day. You should enjoy _____ with a good friend.

♐ Sagittarius (November 22–December 21) If you want to be successful, keep on _____ . Don't feel sorry for _____ last month.

♑ Capricorn (December 22–January 19) A great day for _____ . Avoid _____ before you have more information. _____ is dangerous.

♒ Aquarius (January 20–February 18) You're bored with _____ . Try to get excited about _____ . Avoid _____ .

♓ Pisces (February 19–March 20) Think about _____ something new next weekend. How about _____ with a new friend?

B.

Where do they grow corn?	OR	Where **is** corn **grown?**
They grow corn in Kansas.	OR	Corn **is grown** in Kansas.
Where do they make cars?	OR	Where **are** cars **made?**
They make cars in Michigan.	OR	Cars **are made** in Michigan.

1 **Pete's helping Michael study for a geography test. Ask questions in the passive voice. Then look at the map and answer the questions.**

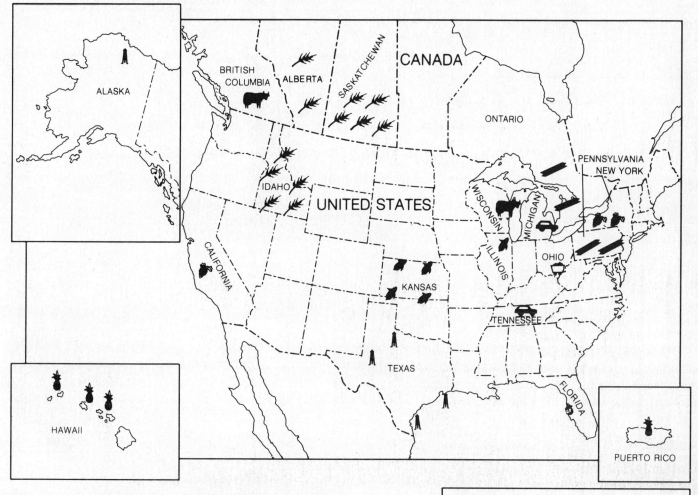

Note: These products are also found in other states and provinces.

LEGEND

cars		oil	
coal		oranges	
corn		pineapples	
dairy products		steel	
grapes		wheat	

1. corn / grow

PETE: Where's corn grown?
MICHAEL: Corn's grown in Illinois.

2. oil / find
3. cars / make
4. coal / mine
5. grapes / grow

6. steel / manufacture
7. oranges / grow
8. dairy products / produce
9. wheat / grow
10. pineapples / grow

2   Now ask and answer questions about your classmates' countries.

A: Is *rice grown* in *Thailand?*
B: Yes, *it is. It's grown* in . . .
   OR   No, *it isn't.*

3   Ken, Steve and Cathy are talking about Ken's new job. Read their conversation and complete it.

STEVE: Don't worry about the job. It's really easy. The doors *are locked* when the
         _____ when the
         1. lock

         warehouse closes at 6:00. Then the alarms _____. All you have to do is make your
                                                   2. set

         rounds.

KEN: It sounds like an easy job.

CATHY: I'm nervous about him working there. Especially at night.

STEVE: Don't worry, Cathy. Nothing valuable _____ in that warehouse. No one will want to
                                              3. keep

         break in. And now the area _____ all night by the police because of all the fires.
                                    4. patrol

KEN: And I'll make more money working on the night shift. How often _____ we _____?
                                                                                              5. pay

STEVE: Checks _____ every week. After your taxes _____, you'll get about $160.00.
                6. give out   7. take out

4   Find out about someone's job.

1. How often / pay
A: How often are you paid?
   OR   How often is your sister paid?
B: Once a month.
   OR   I don't know.
2. checks / mail or give out
3. taxes / deduct
4. How often / raises give
5. job evaluations / do
6. How often / promotions give

5   Talk about neighborhood services.

A: When *is the mail delivered* in your neighborhood?
B: *It's delivered in the morning.*

Student A can use these ideas:

garbage collected	street lights turned on
streets cleaned	electric meters read

PUT IT ALL TOGETHER
Two men are talking. Listen and complete their conversation.

LUKE: Well, is everything all set for Saturday night?

PHIL: Yes. We'll meet you at 1:00 A.M.

LUKE: Which _warehouse_ is it?
      1

PHIL: Number ____. It's on the west side of Palmer Road, south of Warehouse 6.
            2

LUKE: What do you know about the ____?
                                 3

PHIL: There are ____ doors. The main ____ is on the south side. The doors ____ ____ when
                4   5   6   7
the workers go home at 6:00.

LUKE: What about ____?
                 8

PHIL: There are two on the east side and ____ on the west side.
                                         9

LUKE: ____ they all protected ____ alarms?
      10   11

PHIL: Yes, they are. The alarm box ____ located on the right side of the main door.
                                   12

LUKE: What other security is there?

PHIL: Well, there's a ____. His desk is to the left of the main door.
                      13

Now read the conversation and match the numbers on the diagram with these places:

_10_ Palmer Road

____ Warehouse 6

____ main door

____ windows on the east

____ windows on the west

____ security guard's desk

____ alarm box

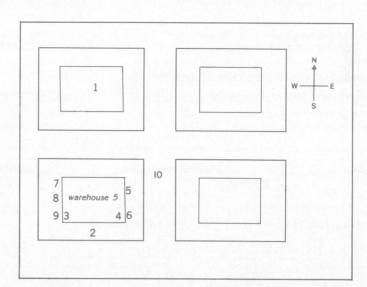

ON YOUR OWN
Think about Angela's dinner party at the beginning of the unit and discuss these questions with your classmates.

1 Do you like inviting people to dinner at your home? At a restaurant?

2 If you go to someone's home for dinner, do you usually bring him or her something? If so, what? Do you usually arrive early, late or exactly on time? What about in your country?

Reading

1 Predicting. The Houston *Herald,* like other newspapers, has sections on different subjects. Look at the article. Which of these sections do you think it came from?

1. Local News
2. Home
3. Business
4. Classified Ads
5. Sports

2 Read this article about apple pie.

The Houston Herald

Cathy's Corner

THE ALL-AMERICAN DESSERT

by Cathy Wilson

Ask any American to name the traditional national dessert and they'll probably say "apple pie." There's even the well-known saying, "It's as American as apple pie," that shows the special
(5) relationship Americans have with this delicious dessert. Why not serve it this summer à la mode— with your favorite flavor of ice cream? It'll make the perfect ending to your Fourth of July celebration.

Among the hundreds of recipes for apple pie,
(10) here's one of mine that's tried and true—an appropiate tribute to the red, white and blue.

Apple Pie

5–7 tart apples
½ cup brown sugar
(15) 1 teaspoon cinnamon
¼ teaspoon nutmeg
1½ tablespoons butter
2 9″-unbaked pie crusts (use your favorite recipe or buy ready-made crusts)

(20) Preheat the oven to 450°F (230°C). Core, peel and slice the apples. Combine the sugar and spices. Mix them with the apples. Line a pie plate with one of the crusts, and fill it with the apple mixture. Dot the mixture with butter. Cover it with the top crust.
(25) Prick the top crust in several places to allow steam to escape.

Bake for 10 minutes at 450°F (230°C). Reduce the heat to 350°F (175°C), and continue baking for 40 minutes or until the pie is done.

3 Comprehension. Say *That's right* or *That's wrong.*

1. Apple pie is a very popular American dessert.
2. If you eat something à la mode, you eat it with ice cream.
3. There are only a few recipes for apple pie.
4. The "red, white and blue" in line 11 probably refers to different flavors of ice cream.
5. According to the recipe, you only have to bake the apple pie for 40 minutes.

4 Putting steps in order. Read these steps for making apple pie. Then put them in the correct order.

a. _____ Fill the pie crust with the apple mixture.
b. _____ Mix the apples with sugar and spices.
c. _____ Turn the oven to 350°F (175°C).
d. __1__ Turn the oven to 450°F (230°C).
e. _____ Cover the mixture with the top crust.
f. _____ Cut the apples into slices.
g. _____ Dot the mixture with butter.
h. _____ Put the pie in the oven.

Writing

Skill: Writing steps in a process
Task: Writing instructions

1 Look at the pictures. They show how to grow an avocado plant. Then read the sentences and put them in the correct order according to the pictures.

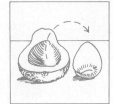 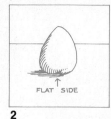 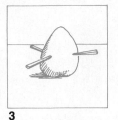   

1   2   3   4   5   6

a. _____ Put three or four toothpicks into the sides of the seed.
b. _____ Cut the avocado in half and remove the seed.
c. _____ Put the jar in a sunny place.
d. _____ Hold the avocado seed so that the flat side is facing down.
e. _____ Fill the jar with water.
f. _____ Place the seed with the toothpicks into the jar.

2 Now read the instructions for growing an avocado plant and complete them by adding the six steps in Exercise 1. Notice how the sequencing words—*first, next, then, after that* and *finally*—help show the order of events.

AVOCADO PLANTS_____

It's not hard to grow an avocado plant. You will need an avocado, a jar about 7 inches tall and 4 inches wide, and some toothpicks. First, _____. Next _____. Then_____. After that,_____ _____. Next_____, resting the toothpicks on the edge of the jar so that only the bottom of the seed is covered by water. Finally,_____.

You won't get avocados from an indoor avocado plant, but you will have a pretty plant to look at.

3 Now write a paragraph explaining how to do something. First, choose one of these topics or a topic of your own.

How to:	
make a glass of iced tea	change a tire
make a cassette recording	hang a picture

Next, list the steps in the correct order. Finally, write your instructions in paragraph form. Be sure to use sequencing words to help indicate the order of events.

For pronunciation exercises for Unit 7, see page 114.

8 Do You Smell Smoke?

1 Ken has just gotten to work. He is talking to Rob, another security guard. Listen to their conversation.

1

KEN: How are things tonight, Rob?

ROB: Very quiet. I'll be ready to go as soon as I punch out. So, how do you like working the night shift?

KEN: It's fine. After three months without a job, any shift is OK with me.

ROB: I know what you mean. You must be glad to have a job again.

KEN: You'd better believe it. How long have you worked here, Rob?

ROB: I was hired right before Christmas last year. The job's not difficult, but I'd like to find something better. It's hard to make ends meet on this salary.

2

KEN: I know. We've got two kids and a mortgage. Luckily, my wife works too. The bad thing is she leaves for work right after I get home.

ROB: Oh, that reminds me. *My* wife asked me to get some things at the Stop and Save. I'd better go now. They close at midnight.

3

KEN: Hey, do you smell smoke?

ROB: Warehouse 5 must be on fire!

KEN: Warehouse 5! My brother Steve's working there. Call the fire department! I'm going to find him!

2 Give a reason for each statement.

1. Ken's happy to have this job.
2. Rob would like to find another job.
3. Ken's glad Cathy works.
4. Rob thinks Warehouse 5 is on fire.

3 Find a word or phrase in the conversation that means:

1. hours you work
2. It's difficult to pay all my bills.
3. given a job
4. money you get for work

4 Warm Up

Complain to a classmate. He or she will sympathize with you.

A: It's hard *being unemployed.*

B: *I know what you mean. Being unemployed is terrible.*

DEVELOP YOUR VOCABULARY

(Student B)
I can sympathize with you.
I know what it's like.
I know how you feel.
. . .

Practice

A.

When As soon as After	Rob **punches out,** he'll leave.	OR	Rob will leave	when as soon as after	he **punches out.**
Before	Rob **leaves,** he'll punch out.	OR	Rob will punch out	before	he **leaves.**

1 What do you think the characters will do later? Make sentences by combining columns A and B. Be sure to change the form of the verbs.

1. As soon as Rob punches out, he'll leave the warehouse.

A

1. As soon as Rob (punch) out, he
2. After he (finish) his test, Michael
3. Tom (write) another story before he
4. When Linda (leave) the office this evening, she
5. This afternoon Ken (leave) for work as soon as Cathy
6. After Pete (get) home today, he

B

a. (go) to baseball practice.
b. (go) to the movies tonight.
c. (get) home.
d. (leave) the warehouse.
e. (visit) Bill.
f. (call) Suzanne.

2 Minh is talking to his wife, Lan, about their plans for the future. Listen to their conversation and put the pictures in the right order.

_____ moving _____ getting raise _____ mother arriving _1_ talking to Angela _____ looking at beds

3 Tell a classmate about something you'd like to buy.

A: I'd like to buy *a car.*
B: When are you going to buy *one?*
A: As soon as *I get my driver's license.*

Student A can use these ideas:

> **As soon as *I* get:**
> a promotion / raise / job / credit card / loan my income tax refund
>
> **As soon as *I*:**
> save enough money
> win the lottery

B.

Another warehouse **was destroyed**	**by** an arsonist. **by** fire.
The firefighters **were called** to the scene.	

1 Read this article from the Houston *Herald* and complete it with the correct forms of the verbs.

The Houston Herald

4th Warehouse Destroyed Security Guards Injured

HOUSTON —Last night another warehouse in the downtown area of Houston _was destroyed_
1. destroy
by fire. The fire department _____to the
2. call
scene at 11:00 P.M. Although they arrived only five minutes later, they were unable to put out the flames. The police suspect that the fire _____
3. start
by an arsonist. Last month three buildings

_____ in the area, and police believe that
4. burn down
this was the work of the same person. This, however, is the first time that anyone _____
5. injure

in the blaze. Two brothers, Ken and Steven Wilson, both security guards on duty at the time,

_____ unconscious outside the burning
6. find
building. They _____to City Hospital,
7. rush
where both _____in satisfactory condition.
8. list

This fire is the most costly so far. In addition to the injuries of the Wilson brothers, valuable paintings worth millions of dollars_____ in the fire.
9. destroy
The paintings, which_____ by the Houston
10. own
Art Museum, were going to be returned to the museum next week.

**2 Angela and her husband, Frank, are talking about what happened to Ken Wilson.
Listen and choose the get-well note they sent Ken in the hospital.**

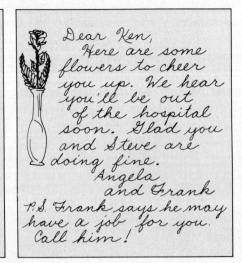

1

2

3

3 Tell a classmate some bad news. He or she will express sympathy.

A: Hey, *Marta*, you look upset. What's the matter?
B: I just got some bad news. *A friend of mine was injured in a car accident.*
A: *I'm sorry to hear that. I hope your friend gets well soon.*
  OR *Was your friend badly hurt?*

Student B can use these ideas:

was/were:	
fired	mugged
laid off	robbed
demoted	hurt

DEVELOP YOUR VOCABULARY

(Student A)
That's:
terrible   a shame
awful   . . .

Just for Fun

4

The Houston Herald

The *Herald* Trivia Quiz

Who? When? What? Where? Why? How much? How many? Can you answer these questions? You'll find the answers at the bottom of the page.

1. *Sunflowers* was painted by
   a. Pablo Picasso
   b. Vincent Van Gogh
   c. Georgia O'Keeffe

2. The Statue of Liberty was dedicated in
   a. 1786
   b. 1886
   c. 1986

3. An igloo is made of
   a. plastic
   b. sand
   c. ice

4. The Great Pyramids are located in
   a. England
   b. Egypt
   c. Ethiopia

5. A churn is used to
   a. make butter
   b. wash clothes
   c. mix paint

6. London Bridge was sold for
   a. $2,500.00
   b. $25,000.00
   c. $2,500,000.00

7. Mandarin Chinese is spoken by about
   a. 100,000 people
   b. 1,000,000 people
   c. 1,000,000,000 people

Answers: 1.b 2.b 3.c 4.b 5.a 6.c 7.c

C.

| Cathy **must be** worried about Ken. She **must not feel** very relaxed. | **Note:** We do not contract *must not* when we use it to make a deduction. |

1 Make deductions by using the words below each picture.

1. Cathy must be worried about Ken.
   She must not feel very relaxed.

1. Cathy / be worried about Ken
   She / feel relaxed

2. Pete / miss Suzanne
   He / be happy

3. Suzanne / be at home
   She / be out

4. Linda / be allergic to flowers
   She / be in Ken's room

5. Michael / be relieved
   Pete / be proud

2 Tell a classmate some good news.

A: I have *good* news. *My sister was given a scholarship.*
B: Oh, that's *wonderful. She* must *be* very *proud.*

Student A can use these ideas:

| **was:** |
| given a raise |
| promoted |
| elected *class president* |
| chosen *as captain of her volleyball team* |

3 Listen to these people. Then make a deduction about each one. Use *must be* and an adjective.

1. He . . .   5. He . . .
2. She . . .   6. She . . .
3. He . . .   7. He . . .
4. She . . .

Just for Fun

4 What deductions can you make about the person who lives in this room? Use *must* and *must not*.

This person must *play baseball*.

Now think about the characters in the story. Whose room do you think this is?

It must be _____'s room.

Life Skills

Food

1 Rob, Ken Wilson's co-worker, is at Stop and Save. He is having trouble finding some of the things on his shopping list. Listen and complete his conversation with a clerk.

ROB: Excuse me. Where can I find _____ _____ ?
                                        1   2

CLERK: In aisle _____ , _____ side, right across from the _____ supplies.
                    3   4   5

ROB: OK. Thanks a lot.

Now look at Rob's shopping list and the floor plan of Stop and Save. Practice asking and giving directions.

orange juice
milk
lettuce
tomatoes
frozen spinach
1 lb. chopped meat
1 dozen eggs
canned peas
bran cereal
spaghetti
tomato sauce

paper towels
toilet paper
laundry detergent

	①			②		③			④			⑤	
Ice Cream		Candy	Paper Products		Pancake Flour		Salad Dressing	Canned Fruit		Spaghetti	Eggs		Fresh Fruits and Vegetables
Frozen Food		Baby Food		Cleaning Supplies	Cereal		Catsup	Juices		Tomato Sauces	Dairy Products		
Meats		Baking Needs	Detergent	Shoe Polish	Sugar		Pickles	Canned Vegetables		Soup			

2 Rob is deciding which products to buy. Look at the products and discuss if one is a better buy than the other. Give a reason for your opinion.

1. A: I think Marvel detergent is a better buy. The bottle is bigger, and the price is the same as Wonder.
   B: But Wonder has 64 ounces of detergent, and Marvel has only 57 ounces.
   OR   I agree.

1. $4.59

$4.59

2. 55¢

2 for 97¢

3. 41¢

47¢

4. $2.69 $1.39   5. $0.99 $2.07

3 **Rob has several coupons. Look at them. Then read each statement and say** *That's right, That's wrong* **or** *I don't know.*

1. a. Rob can only use this coupon in Stop and Save stores.
   b. He can buy as many rolls as he wants with this coupon.
   c. He can use this coupon next year.
   d. He saves 10¢ a roll when he uses this coupon.

2. a. Rob can only save on Miller's brand spaghetti.
   b. If he uses this coupon, he'll get one pound of spaghetti.
   c. He can only buy two packages of spaghetti with this coupon.
   d. He can use this coupon next year.

3. a. Rob can only use this coupon in Stop and Save stores.
   b. He has to use this coupon before 1991.
   c. He'll save 25¢ if he uses this coupon.
   d. If he buys two bottles of Rosa's spaghetti sauce, he'll save 50¢.

ON YOUR OWN
Discuss these questions with your classmates.

1 Where do you shop for food? In a large supermarket? In small stores? At a street market? What are some advantages and disadvantages of supermarkets?

2 Do you ever use coupons? Do you think coupons really save you money?

3 Where can people buy food in your country? When are the stores or markets open? Do people use coupons?

For pronunciation exercises for Unit 8, see page 115.

REVIEW 4

1 Complete this conversation with gerunds.

A: Do you enjoy _playing_ tennis?
         1. play

B: Yes. _____ tennis is really a lot of fun. Unfortunately, I'm not very good at _____
        2. play   3. hit
   the ball.

A: Be patient. _____ good at a sport takes time.
               4. become

B: I know. But I look forward to _____ play a good game one day. Do you play?
                                 5. be able to

A: No, but I'm interest in _____ .
                           6. learn

B: Well, how do you feel about _____ with me?
                               7. practice

A: Sounds like a good idea. As long as I don't have to worry about _____ .
                                                                   8. win

B: Don't worry. _____ fun is the most important thing.
                9. have

A: _____ in shape will be good for us too.
   10. get

2 Rewrite these sentences in the passive voice.

1. They grow rice in India.

Rice is grown in India.

2. They produce televisions in Japan.
3. They mine gold in the Soviet Union.
4. They make leather products in Italy.

5. They manufacture shoes in Brazil.
6. They mine diamonds in South Africa.
7. They manufacture steel in South Korea.
8. They produce cars in Yugoslavia.
9. They grow pineapples in Thailand.

3 Complete this magazine article with the active or passive form of the verbs.

Have you ever wondered where Christmas trees come from? Many of them _are grown_ on
                                                                    1. grow
Christmas tree farms in New England. From there, they _____ all over the United States. Often they
                                                       2. send
_____ two or even three months before Christmas.
3. cut
Then they _____ in water so they won't dry out.
          4. put

Growers sometimes even _____ them in lakes
                       5. keep
or ponds until they're _____ to customers.
                       6. send
Therefore, you must be very careful when you
_____ your tree. Look at the trunk. If it _____
7. choose   8. be
black near the bottom, that _____ it was cut a
                            9. mean
while ago and it may dry out quickly.

4 Complete each sentence with your own information.

1. I'll stop studying English as soon as _____ .
2. Before I _____ , I'll have to save more money.
3. After _____ , I'll have dinner.

4. I'll be glad when _____ .
5. As soon as _____ , I'll buy another one.

74

5 Complete this conversation between Rob and his wife, Liz. Use the passive form of the verbs.

ROB: Hi, Liz. Sorry I'm late, but there was another fire in one of the warehouses.

LIZ: Oh, no! _Was_ anyone _hurt_ ?
1. hurt

ROB: Yes. The new guard, Ken, and his brother _____ .
2. hurt

LIZ: How? What happened?

ROB: I'm not sure. While I was calling the fire department, Ken rushed to the warehouse to

rescue his brother. Later, both men _____ unconscious in front of the building. Then
3. find

they _____ to the hospital. That's all I know.
4. take

LIZ: _____ their families _____ ?
5. tell

ROB: I'm sure they were.

LIZ: And what happened to the warehouse?

ROB: It _____ by the fire.
6. destroy

6 Can you remember the story? According to the story, these statements are wrong. Correct them using the passive.

1. The fire destroyed a restaurant.

A restaurant wasn't destroyed. A warehouse was.

2. Steve started the fire.

The fire wasn't started by Steve. It was started by the arsonist.

3. The police found Rob unconscious.
4. The security guards put the fire out.
5. The police rushed the arsonist to the hospital.
6. The fire destroyed some valuable furniture.
7. Cathy wrote the newspaper article about the fire.

7 Make deductions with *must* or *must not*. Use the word or phrase in parentheses.

1. He's carrying a guidebook and has a camera around his neck. (tourist)

He must be a tourist.

2. She's only fifteen, and she's in college. (smart)
3. I smell smoke, and I can hear a fire engine. (fire)
4. He's had five accidents in the past four months. (good driver)
5. He's still in the hospital. (well)
6. She buys the newspaper every day and looks at the employment ads. (new job)
7. Everyone is wearing sweaters and jackets outside. (cool)
8. No one finished reading that book. (interesting)

8 Put these words in the correct order.

1. frightening fires be must fighting

Fighting fires must be frightening.

2. I go as as to I'll store finish letter this the soon
3. leave you'll before have to you out punch
4. guard reported fire was security by the the

1 Officer Brady asked Ken Wilson to come to the police station. Listen to their conversation.

1

BRADY: Thanks for coming, Mr. Wilson.

KEN: Well, I wanted to talk to you. We *must* get the people who did this.

BRADY: But *you* mustn't get involved. We can investigate more easily by ourselves. Just tell me everything you can remember about the fire.

2

KEN: I don't know where to begin. It all happened so quickly.

BRADY: Well, just begin at the beginning.

KEN: OK. I smelled smoke and ran as fast as I could to Warehouse 5.

BRADY: Yes, go on. What did you do then?

KEN: I didn't know what to do. I just kept calling my brother's name.

3

BRADY: Did you see or hear anyone?

KEN: No, it was too smoky. I couldn't see anything. But I heard a woman's voice.

BRADY: A *woman's* voice? Are you positive?

KEN: Yes, but I couldn't make out what she was saying. Then someone hit me hard over the head. The next thing I knew, I was in the hospital.

2 Correct the information.

1. Officer Brady wants Ken to work with the police.
2. Ken was working in Warehouse 5.
3. Ken saw a woman in the warehouse.
4. Ken woke up in the warehouse.

4 Warm Up

Thank a classmate for doing something.

A: Thanks for *helping me with my homework*. I really appreciate it.

B: *You're welcome.* I was glad to do it.

3 Find a word or phrase in the conversation that means:

1. have to
2. understand
3. sure
4. without anyone else

DEVELOP YOUR VOCABULARY

(Student B)

That's OK.   My pleasure.

Sure thing.   Don't mention it.

Anytime.   . . .

Practice

A.

> It all happened so **quickly**.

Spelling note: Regular adverbs

quick + ly ⟶ quickly
immediate + ly ⟶ immediately
capable + ly ⟶ capably
beautiful + ly ⟶ beautifully
happy + ly ⟶ happily

Irregular adverbs

Adjective	Adverb
hard	hard
fast	fast
good	well

1 Talk about each picture by using the words in the box.

slow	incorrect	~~impolite~~
fast	sloppy	

1. The child spoke impolitely.

1. speak

2. be dressed

3. answer the question

4. drive

5. move

2 Review and Build

Read Frank and Angela's conversation and complete it. The adjective form is given. Change it to the adverb form when necessary.

FRANK: I feel ___*terrible*___ about the fire, Angela.
                1. terrible

ANGELA: How bad was the damage, Frank?

FRANK: _____. The fire department fought _____ to save the building, but they
        2. awful   3. courageous
couldn't. I don't know what to tell the museum board.

ANGELA: You shouldn't feel _____. You acted _____. You put the paintings in a
                        4. guilty   5. responsible
_____ place.
    6. safe

FRANK: I know. But why wasn't I more _____?
                             7. careful

ANGELA: What did the insurance company say?

FRANK: They said they'll try _____ to send the money _____, but before they do,
                    8. hard   9. quick
they have to make a _____ investigation.
       10. complete

3 Tell a classmate about something you wish you could do.

A: I wish I could *speak English fluently*. What about you?
B: I wish I could *type fast*.

B.

> Michael writes **more neatly than** Cindy.
> He works **harder than** her.

1 Michael's teacher is comparing two homework papers. Look at the papers and use the words in the box to compare them like this:

A: Who writes more neatly?
B: Michael writes more neatly than Cindy.

write neatly	spell accurately
write grammatically	write better
work hard	write creatively

Rewrite this, Cindy!

My Sumer vacation
         by Cindy Lewis
  I done meny things
On my vacation. I had a
Very good time. I am sorry
that Skool has Started agin.
I went to the Playgroun,
I went to the pull Pool.

1

My Visit to Outer Space Excellent!
        by Michael Gómez
    Last night I had a fantastic
dream. I dreamt I visited the
planet of Saturn. The dream started
when I was walking in the woods
and I saw a spaceship. While
I watched through the bushes,
I saw some little people come
out of the spaceship.

2

2 Review and Build

An editor from the Houston *Sun* wants to hire a reporter. Two of Angela's students from her night class have applied for the job. The editor is calling Angela to get references about them. Listen to their conversation and make notes about each student.

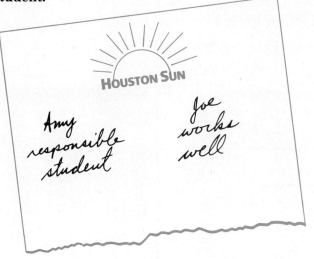

Now talk to a classmate and decide if the editor should hire Amy or Joe.

A: I think the editor should hire *Amy. She's more responsible* than *Joe.*

B: I agree. *Amy's a hard worker.*
   OR   Yes, but *Joe writes better.*

A: But . . .

C.

> Ken didn't know **where to begin** his story.
> He didn't know **what to do.**

1 Talk about each person's problem.

1. A: What's the matter with Johnny?
   B: He doesn't know what to do now.

2 Michael Gómez is having a problem. He's asking a woman for advice. Listen to their conversation. Then read the sentences below and decide if they are right or wrong.

1. The woman knows how to use the machine.
2. Michael knows how much money to put in the machine.
3. Michael knows where to put the money.
4. Michael knows what to do after he puts the money in the machine.

Now listen to the conversation again and choose the machine that Michael and the woman are talking about.

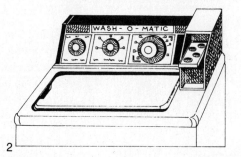

3 Ask a classmate for advice about a problem.

A: I have a problem. I don't know *what to buy my sister-in-law for her birthday.*

B: How about *a record? Everyone likes music.*

You can use these ideas:

where / buy *Mexican ingredients*
how / find *a good doctor*
who / complain to about *my broken sink*

D.

The police **must find** the arsonist.		
Ken	**must not** **mustn't**	**get** involved.
	doesn't have to	**see** Officer Brady again.

Note: *You mustn't do that* means *You can't do that* (because it's wrong or bad). *You don't have to do that* means *You can do it if you want* (but it isn't necessary).

1 Review and Build

After speaking to Officer Brady, Ken went to see his doctor. Listen to their conversation and check the things that Ken *must* do, *mustn't* do and *doesn't have to* do.

	must	mustn't	doesn't have to
1. get a lot of rest	✓		
2. stay in bed			
3. go back to work			
4. go back for a checkup			
5. make another appointment			

Now talk about what the doctor told Ken.

1. A: What did the doctor tell Ken about getting rest?
   B: She said he must get a lot of rest.

2 Michael is still at the laundromat. He's reading the washing instructions on the clothing labels. Look at each label. Say what you *must* or *don't have to* do.

1. You don't have to iron it.
   OR You must dry it on low.

> **PERMANENT PRESS**
> **NO IRONING NEEDED**
> **DRY ON LOW**
>
> 1

> **CARE INSTRUCTIONS**
>
> **WARM WATER ONLY**
>
> 2

> **DRY CLEAN ONLY**
>
> 3

> **CARE INSTRUCTIONS**
>
> **DRY CLEAN or HAND WASH**
>
> 4

> TURN GARMENT INSIDE OUT.
> MACHINE WASH MEDIUM.
> DO NOT BLEACH.
> TUMBLE DRY LOW HEAT OR
> HAND WASH WARM - LAY FLAT TO DRY
>
> 5

PUT IT ALL TOGETHER

Bill asked Linda to have coffee with him. Listen to the conversation and complete the statements.

1. Bill thanked Linda for coming
   a. alone.
   b. so fast.
   c. to interview him.

2. Bill told Linda he doesn't know
   a. what to do.
   b. who to talk to.
   c. when to leave.

3. Bill told Linda where to find
   a. another reporter.
   b. the man who spoke to him.
   c. a good restaurant.

4. Bill told Linda to go to the diner
   a. alone.
   b. with another reporter.
   c. with the police.

5. Bill says the diner isn't
   a. crowded.
   b. safe.
   c. famous.

Now look at these advertisements. Which one do you think is an ad for Rosie's Diner?

ELEGANT CANDLELIGHT DINING
Romantic Setting

Open for Dinner Tuesday - Sunday
RESERVATIONS REQUIRED

1

Family Restaurant
Children Welcome

HAVE YOUR NEXT PARTY HERE
Open for Lunch and Dinner

2

Great Homemade Food

Low Prices

Daily Specials

OPEN 24 HOURS

3

ON YOUR OWN

Think about some of the problems people had in this unit and discuss the following questions with your classmates.

1 When you first came to this country (or started this class), what were some things you didn't know how to do? How did you solve these problems?

2 What are some problems that a foreigner might have in your country? What advice would you give him or her?

Reading

1 **Skimming. Look quickly at these two restaurant reviews. Which restaurant does the reviewer like better? How do you know? Which restaurant is more expensive?**

2 **Now read the reviews.**

The Houston Herald

Eating Out ——— by Cathy Wilson

*	fair	$	inexpensive
**	good	$$	moderate
***	very good	$$$	expensive
****	excellent	$$$$	very expensive

Credit Cards: **Amex** American Express, **V** Visa, **MC** MasterCard, **DC** Diner's Club

ᙕ Accessible to the handicapped

SZECHUAN PALACE **

The Szechuan Palace is a new restaurant in downtown Houston which serves spicy Chinese cuisine. The food is generally good, but the
(5) decor leaves much to be desired. The room is very dark, and the tables are much too close together.

In spite of the lack of comfort, the Szechuan Palace is still worth a visit. I heartily recommend the chili-pepper chicken, the Szechuan green beans and
(10) the peas with crabmeat sauce.

Open for lunch and dinner Tuesday through Sunday. 3205 Montrose. Reservations necessary Friday and Saturday nights.
555–4892/$$/Amex·V·MC/ᙕ

(15) **HAMBURGER HAVEN** ****

Since it opened just six months ago, Hamburger Haven has become one of the most popular lunch spots in downtown Houston. Although it is self-service, it looks much more like a café than a typical
(20) fast-food eatery. The large number of plants creates a cheery atmosphere.

The food at Hamburger Haven is as good as the decor. They serve ten different types of hamburgers including Taco Burgers with jalapeño cheese, Pizza
(25) Burgers with mozzarella cheese and tomato sauce, and Alpine Burgers with swiss cheese and mushrooms. For those who are dieting, there is a well-stocked salad bar.

Open for lunch Monday through Saturday. 4309 Broad.
555–9216/$/No CC

---

3 **Comprehension. Answer these questions. If you don't understand a word in the reviews, try to guess its meaning without looking in the dictionary.**

1. What does the reviewer think of the decor at the Szechuan Palace?
2. How is the food at the Szechuan Palace?
3. Do they accept reservations at the Szechuan Palace?
4. How can you pay for your meal at the Szechuan Palace?
5. Who serves the meals at Hamburger Haven?
6. When is Hamburger Haven open?
7. How can you pay for your meal at Hamburger Haven?
8. Which restaurant has facilities for the handicapped?

4 Guessing the meaning from context. Match the words in column A with their definitions in column B.

A	B
1. cuisine	a. usual
2. spicy	b. type of food
3. decor	c. restaurant
4. lack	d. to have a lot of
5. typical	e. the way a room looks
6. eatery	f. hot in flavor
7. to be well stocked	g. absence

5 Discussion. What do you think? Discuss these questions with your classmates.

1. The decor of a restaurant is very important to this reviewer. Is it important to you? Why?

2. Which of these restaurants would you rather eat in? Why?

Writing

Skill: Describing
Task: Writing a review

1 You are going to write a review of a place you have eaten in recently. It can be a restaurant, a diner, the school cafeteria or someone's home.

Think about the place and make notes about it as you answer these questions.

1. Is it big or small? Crowded or empty?
2. How is it decorated?
   a. Are there pictures on the walls?
   b. Are there flowers on the tables?
   c. What does the furniture look like?
3. What's the atmosphere like?
   a. Does it make you feel happy? Depressed?
   b. Is it warm and comfortable or cold and sterile?
   c. Is it noisy or quiet?
4. What kind of food do they serve there?
5. How is the food?
   a. What is the best dish?
   b. The worst?
6. Is it expensive?
7. What's the best thing about the place? The worst?

2 Read the two restaurant reviews again. Then use your notes to write your review about the place you ate in.

For pronunciation exercises for Unit 9, see page 115.

1 Linda went to Rosie's Diner to find the man Bill told her about. Listen to the conversation.

1

LINDA: Tom, this is Linda. Is Angela there?

TOM: No, she isn't. She just left for the airport. What's up?

LINDA: Well, I'm at Rosie's Diner on Fulton. The guy Bill described is here. I'm going to follow him when he leaves. I just wanted someone to know.

TOM: You should let the police do . . .

LINDA: I've got to go—he's leaving. Bye!

2

CAROL: Do you know when Phil's coming?

LUKE: He said 4:00.

CAROL: Well, it's 4:15 now. I wonder where he is.

LUKE: Take it easy. He'll show up.

3

PHIL: Look who I found eavesdropping.

LINDA: Carol!

CAROL: Is she alone?

PHIL: Yeah, I think so.

CAROL: I sent you that letter to make you stop snooping. You should've listened, Linda.

LINDA: You . . . . you started those fires. Why?

CAROL: I guess I can tell you now. You won't have a chance to tell anyone else.

2 Say *That's right, That's wrong* or *I don't know*.

1. Linda spoke to Angela.
2. Angela went to Dallas.
3. Linda told Tom where she was going.
4. Linda found the arsonists.
5. Carol isn't afraid of Linda.

4 Warm Up

Pretend you are upset about something. A classmate will try to calm you down and make a suggestion.

A: I'm really upset *that I didn't get a raise.*

B: *Take it easy.* Maybe you should *talk to your boss again.*

3 Find a word or phrase in the conversation that means:

1. looking into someone's life without permission
2. want to know
3. What's happening?
4. listening secretly to a conversation

DEVELOP YOUR VOCABULARY

Calm down.	Relax.
Don't be upset.	. . .

Practice

A.

Linda	should have should've	**called** the police.
	shouldn't have gone to the diner alone.	

Note: *Should've* is pronounced "should of." *Shouldn't have* is pronounced "shouldn't of."

1 Talk about what the people *should have* or *shouldn't have* done.

1. Linda should've called the police.

1

2

3

4

5

6

7

8

2 **Tom is telling Pete about Linda's phone call. Listen to their conversation. Then choose the picture that shows what Pete thinks Tom should have done.**

1

2

3

3 **Review and Build**

Carol is explaining her plan to Linda. Read their conversation and complete it with *should/shouldn't* or *should have/shouldn't have* and the correct form of the verb.

CAROL: You <u>*shouldn't have come*</u> here, Linda.
    1. come

LINDA: *You* _____ those paintings. Why did you do it?
    2. destroy

CAROL: Money. You're not rich. You _____ how it feels to need money all the time.
    3. know

LINDA: But how can you make money from paintings you burned?

CAROL: The paintings *weren't* burned.

LINDA: But the police found pieces of canvas and picture frames in the fire.

CAROL: They _____ them more carefully. The paintings that were burned were not the
    4. examine

originals. They were worthless. We took the real ones out of the warehouse before we

started the fire.

LINDA: And all those other fires?

CAROL: We didn't want this fire to get special attention. Maybe we _____ so many, but it's
    5. start

too late now.

LINDA: Well, you sound very confident, but maybe you _____. What are you going to do
    6. be

with me?

CAROL: Well, I _____ you this, but there's going to be another fire. This time in Warehouse 6.
    7. tell

Unfortunately, someone's going to die this time. You _____ to my warning note.
    8. listen

You _____ your investigation.
    9. continue

4 **Ask a classmate to tell you about something he or she regrets.**

A: What do you regret about your life?
B: I think I *should* have *become a police officer*. What
    about you?
A: Oh, I *shouldn't* have *gotten married so young*.
    OR   I don't really have any regrets.

B.

Where is she?		where **she is.**
When's he coming?		when **he's coming.**
What does it mean?	I wonder	what **it means.**
How many people know?		how many **people know.**
Is it true?		if **it's true.**

1 What is Carol Fullerton thinking? Begin with these words:

1. She wonders . . .

She wonders when Phil's coming.

2. She wants to know . . .
3. She doesn't understand . . .
4. She wants to know . . .
5. She wonders . . .

When's Phil coming? Where is he? Why is he late? Is he in trouble? What does Linda really know?

Now say what Tom is thinking. Begin with these words:

6. He wonders . . .
7. He doesn't know . . .
8. He wants to know . . .
9. He doesn't understand . . .

Where's Linda now?
Is she still at Rosie's?
Is she in trouble?
Why does Linda always do things alone?

2 It's later. Look at Linda. What do you think she wonders? Complete her thoughts.

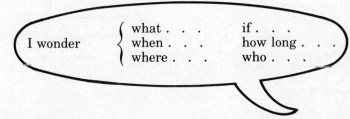

I wonder
what . . .   if . . .
when . . .   how long . . .
where . . .   who . . .

3 Express curiosity about your future.

A: I wonder *where I'll be in ten years.*
B: I wonder *if I'll get married.*
C: . . .

| Do you know | what **it means?**
why **they did** it?
who **she is?**
if **it's** here? |

4 Ask a classmate one of the questions below. Begin with *Do you know* . . . ? If your classmate doesn't know the answer, he or she will tell you where to get the information.

Some places to find information:

dictionary	yellow pages
thesaurus	train schedule
encyclopedia	bus map
almanac	TV schedule
atlas	newspaper

1. What country exports the most rice?

A: Do you know *what country exports the most rice?*

B: I'm sorry, I don't know. Why don't you look *in an almanac?* OR *I think it's China.*

2. What does *residential* mean?
3. Can turkeys fly?
4. What bus can I take to the library?
5. Are there any good movies in town?
6. What's on TV tonight?
7. Where's Sri Lanka?
8. What's another word for *agree?*
9. Is there a bicycle repair shop in town?
10. What's the weather going to be like tomorrow?

5 Ask a classmate something about his or her country.

A: Do you know *what Thailand's most important export is?*

B: Sure. *It's rice.*
  OR Sorry. I don't know.

Student A can use these ideas:

population	average income
major industries	yearly rainfall
major exports	

6 Linda has told the criminals that her friends at the *Herald* are going to be worried. Carol wants her to call and tell them she's fine. Listen to the conversation and complete it.

CAROL: Now you're going to call the *Herald.*

LINDA: But I have no idea **what** ___ ___ ___ ___.
  <small>1   2   3   4</small>

CAROL: I'm sure you'll think of something. They must wonder where ___ ___ and why
  <small>5   6</small>
  ___ ___ ___ them again. But you'd better not try to do anything funny.
  <small>7   8   9</small>

LINDA: OK. *(She dials)* Hello. Mr. Tran? This is Linda Smith. Can you tell me if ___
  <small>10</small>
  ___ ?
  <small>11</small>

MINH: Angela's out of town for a week. Didn't you know that?

LINDA: Yes, I did. She must want to know why ___ ___ ___ ___ ___
  <small>12   13   14   15   16</small>
  today. Please tell her that I'm not sure if ___ ___ ___ ___ meet her at
  <small>17   18   19   20</small>
  6:00 at El Fuego. My sister's sick, and I have to see her right away.

MINH: What's going on, Linda? Are you in . . .

LINDA: Thank you, Mr. Tran.

Life Skills

Transportation

1 **Angela flew to Chicago. A few weeks before, she called Northeastern Airlines to make a reservation. Listen to part of her conversation and complete it.**

AGENT: Northeastern.

ANGELA: Hello. I'd like to _make_ (1) a round-trip _______ (2) on one of your flights from Houston to Chicago.

AGENT: OK. When would you like to _______ (3)?

ANGELA: On July _______ (4).

AGENT: And the _______ (5) flight?

ANGELA: July _______ (6).

AGENT: What _______ (7) of day would you like to leave?

ANGELA: In the _______ (8).

AGENT: Well, we have a _______ (9) flight and an _______ (10).

ANGELA: I'd prefer the _______ (11) one. And coming back on the 18th, I'd like a morning _______ (12) too.

AGENT: How about one leaving Chicago at _______ (13) A.M., arriving in Houston at _______ (14)?

ANGELA: That sounds fine. Can you tell me _______ (15) the fare _______ (16)?

AGENT: It's _______ (17) round trip.

ANGELA: I _______ (18) if I can make my seat reservation now too.

AGENT: Certainly. Do you _______ (19) smoking or non-smoking?

ANGELA: _______ (20).

AGENT: _______ (21) or aisle?

ANGELA: _______ (22), please.

AGENT: Please hold on while I check the computer.

Now look at these boarding passes and choose which one is Angela's.

	1	2	3	4
	Northeastern Airlines	Northeastern Airlines	Northeastern Airlines	Northeastern Airlines
NAME OF PASSENGER	Lentini/AMS	Lentini/AMS	Lentini/AMS	Lentini/AMS
FROM	Houston Tx	Houston Tx	Houston Tx	Houston Tx
TO	Chicago Il	Chicago Il	Chicago Il	Chicago Il
CARRIER	Northeastern	Northeastern	Northeastern	Northeastern
FLIGHT	400	400	400	400
DATE	11 July	11 July	11 July	11 July
TIME	930 A	1115 P	930 A	930 A
SEAT	Unassigned	5F 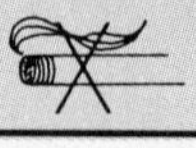	5F 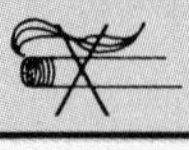	5F 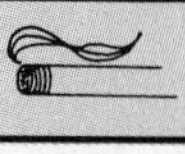

2 When Angela got to the airport she looked at the flight monitor.

Northeastern Airlines

FLT	DEPARTING FOR	SCHED	STATUS	GATE
321	Dallas	7:30 a	On time	5A
604	San Francisco	8:15 a	On time	13B
110	New York	9:00 a	Now boarding	12A
400	Chicago	9:30 a	On time	11A
211	Washington	9:45 a	Delayed	21B
421	Detroit	10:21 a	Cancelled	7B
618	Miami	10:45 a	On time	18A
342	Toronto	11:30 a	On time	9B
701	Pittsburgh	12:00 p	Delayed	6B

Look at the monitor. Find out about the flights, like this:

YOU: Can you tell me what time the flight to Detroit leaves?
AGENT: I'm sorry, but it's been canceled.

Just for Fun

3 At the airport there are many symbols. Match the symbols in column A with the words in column B.

A

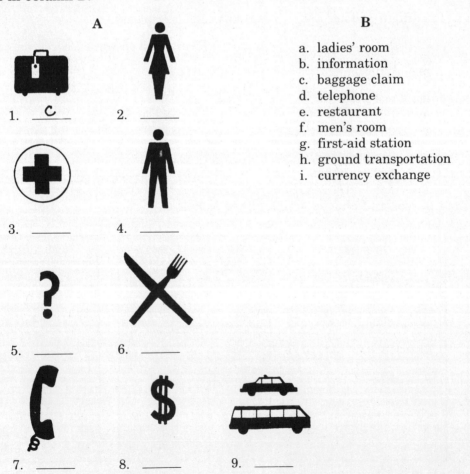

1. _c_   2. ___

3. ___   4. ___

5. ___   6. ___

7. ___   8. ___   9. ___

B

a. ladies' room
b. information
c. baggage claim
d. telephone
e. restaurant
f. men's room
g. first-aid station
h. ground transportation
i. currency exchange

4 **Angela just asked someone for directions. Read the directions she was given. Then look at the map and decide where Angela wanted to go.**

ANGELA: Excuse me. Can you tell me where _____ is?

CLERK: Yes. Go down this hall to the information booth. Turn left and walk to the telephones.

The _____ is to the right of the phones.

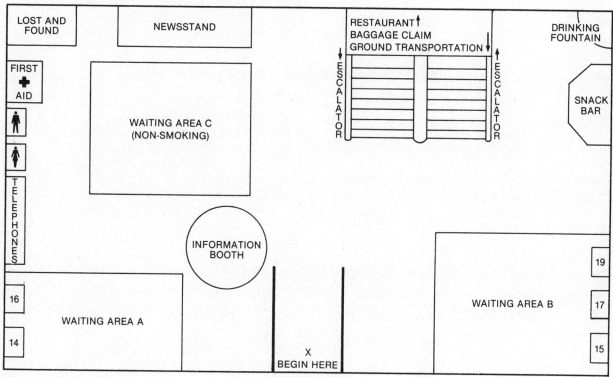

Now use the airport map and practice asking for and giving directions.

5 **Listen to the announcements and choose the correct answers.**

1. The passenger should
   a. call José López on the phone.
   b. board flight 24.
   c. go to the information booth near gate 24.

2. Angela can board now because
   a. her seat number is 5F.
   b. she uses a cane to walk.
   c. she is flying to Chicago.

3. James Walski
   a. is meeting someone at the airport.
   b. must go to the information booth.
   c. is going to a party.

4. A passenger with seat 35F should
   a. go to the information booth.
   b. board now.
   c. wait for another announcement.

5. This announcement was made
   a. in the airport terminal.
   b. in the airplane.
   c. in the airport restaurant.

ON YOUR OWN
Discuss these questions with your classmates.

1 How do you prefer to travel from one city to another (car, bus, train, boat, plane)?

2 What are some advantages and disadvantages of different types of long-distance transportation?

For pronunciation exercises for Unit 10, see page 116.

REVIEW 5

1 Complete this chart with the correct adjectives or adverbs.

Adjective	Adverb		Adjective	Adverb
1. slow	_slowly_	6. _____	sloppily
2. _____	impolitely	7. terrible	_____
3. good	_____	8. _____	carefully
4. hard	_____	9. quick	_____
5. _____	fast	10. grammatical	_____

2 Complete these sentences with words from Exercise 1. Use a word only once.

1. I can't read this letter. Brad writes very _sloppily_.
2. *John walk* is not a _____ sentence.
3. Angela walks a little _____ because she hurt her leg.
4. There was a _____ storm last night, and one of the trees in our yard fell down.
6. You shouldn't be _____ to anyone.
5. Don't worry. I'll be done soon. I work very _____ .

7. If you work _____ , you won't make mistakes.
8. Linda works very _____ . She even works on weekends.
9. Tom plays the piano _____ . He's very talented.
10. The Bullet train is very _____ . It travels about 130 miles per hour.

3 Write sentences about yourself using these adjectives and adverbs.

1. slow
2. fast
3. well
4. carefully
5. sloppy
6. hard

4 Michael is learning how to type in school. Look at the results of his typing test and of Cindy's typing test. Then compare Michael's and Cindy's typing. Use the words to the right and *than*.

Michael	Cindy
40 words per minute 2 mistakes	50 words per minute 10 mistakes

1. more slowly
Michael types more slowly than Cindy.
2. faster
3. more accurately
4. better

5 For each item, compare the two things or people. Use the verbs and adverbs in parentheses.

1. an airplane / a car (go fast)

An airplane goes faster than a car.

2. a two-year old / a ten-year old (speak grammatically)

3. a bicycle / a motorcycle (move slowly)
4. adults / children (act responsibly)
5. cats / dogs (climb trees well)

6 Lan Tran wants to take the train to Dallas. She has a lot of questions. Change her questions to statements using *I don't know* and an infinitive.

1. Which train should I take?

I don't know which train to take.

2. How much do I have to pay?

3. When should I leave?
4. Who should I ask for information?
5. Where should I wait?

7 Pete is talking to Michael. Complete their conversation with *must, mustn't* or *don't have to.*

MICHAEL: I *don't have to* take this medicine, Dad, do I?

1

PETE: Yes. You _____ take your medicine, or you won't get better.

2

MICHAEL: Well, can I go out?

PETE: No, the doctor said that you _____ go out until tomorrow.

3

MICHAEL: Do I have to stay in bed?

PETE: No, you _____ stay in bed, but you _____ stay home and rest.

4   5

8 Read these situations. Then write two sentences about each one. Tell what the person *should have* and *shouldn't have* done.

1. Michael failed his English test.

He should've studied more.
He shouldn't have watched so much TV.

2. Brad bought an expensive car, and now he can't pay for it.

3. Pete's brother, Sam, married Paula because she was rich. Now Sam's very unhappy.
4. Cathy's sister, Miriam, left school when she was 16. Now she can't find a job.
5. Tom's wallet was stolen last night, and he had to walk home five miles because he didn't have bus fare.

9 Make sentences by combining the phrase and the question.

1. I wonder . . .
   How can I get to Chicago?

I wonder how I can get to Chicago.

2. Can you tell me . . .
   Where is the post office?
3. She doesn't know . . .
   Who is the prime minister of England?
4. Do you know . . .
   What time will he be back?
5. We would like to know . . .
   What are your plans?

6. Please tell her . . .
   When are you leaving?
7. I wonder . . .
   Is he American?
8. Would you let me know . . .
   How much does the gift cost?
9. I'm not sure . . .
   When is the class?
10. He needs to find out . . .
    Where does she live?

Just for Fun

10 Unscramble the letters to make words. Then match the words in column A with their opposites in column B.

	A			B	
1.	d.	woylls	*slowly*	a.	daylb	
2.	___	ipolte	_____	b.	yopillsp	
3.	___	lewl	_____	c.	sweor	
4.	___	ralyucfel	_____	d.	saft	*fast*
5.	___	teebrt	_____	e.	teimilop	

Something's Up

1 Minh is talking to Cathy at the *Herald*. Listen to their conversation.

1

MINH: I got a very strange phone call from Linda just now.

CATHY: Really? What was strange about it?

MINH: Well, first of all, she asked me if Angela was here.

CATHY: You're kidding! She must know that Angela's out of town. After all, she's been staying with her!

2

MINH: I know. And then she kept calling me "Mr. Tran." Something's up, and I don't like how it sounds.

CATHY: I think you're right. She must be in danger.

MINH: I wonder if she was trying to give me a secret message.

3

CATHY: What else did she say?

MINH: She said she couldn't meet Angela at some restaurant . . . because her sister was sick.

CATHY: Her sister? Linda's an only child!

MINH: We've got to do something!

CATHY: You're right. We'd better call Officer Brady right away.

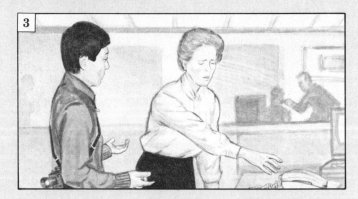

2 Give a reason for these facts.

1. Minh thinks Linda's phone call was strange.
2. Linda should know that Angela's out of town.
3. Linda called Minh "Mr. Tran."
4. Cathy wants to call Officer Brady.

3 Find a word or phrase in the conversation that means:

1. You're not serious.
2. without brothers or sisters
3. away from home
4. Something's wrong.

4 Warm Up

Tell a classmate something that sounds unbelievable. He or she will express disbelief.

A: *I just won $1,000,000 in the lottery.*

B: *You're kidding!*

A: *Yeah,* I'm just kidding.

OR *No, I'm serious. I really did.*

DEVELOP YOUR VOCABULARY

(Student B)

I don't believe it!   Oh, come on.

You're joking!   Are you serious?

You're pulling my leg!   . . .

Practice

A.

"My sister**'s** sick," she said.	She said her* sister **was** sick.	she had = she'd
"We**'re** leaving soon," he said.	He said they* **were** leaving soon.	she would = she'd
"I**'ve** left a note," she said.	She said she* **had** left a note.	
"I**'ll** buy a new car," he said.	He said he* **would** buy a new car.	
"I **can't** meet Angela," she said.	She said she* **couldn't** meet Angela.	

*Note the pronoun changes.

1 Carol, Phil, Luke and Linda are talking. Listen to their conversations and complete them. Then report what each person said.

1. Carol said it was late. Phil said . . .

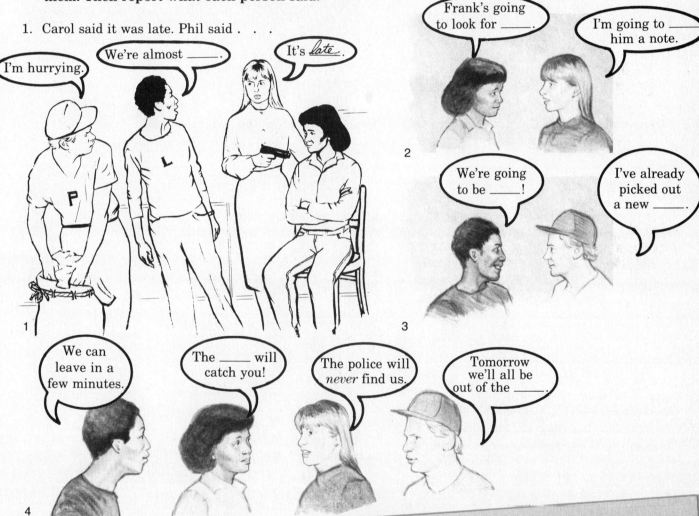

2 Carol went to the museum to get some things. She left a note for Frank on his desk. Read the note and report her lies, like this:

Carol said her mother was sick, but she isn't. She also said . . .

Dear Frank,
My mother is very sick. I have to go to Austin. I'm leaving immediately. I'll be back in a few days. I'm sorry about this.
– Carol

3 While Carol was in Frank's office, she answered the telephone. Listen to the conversation and complete the message Carol left for Frank.

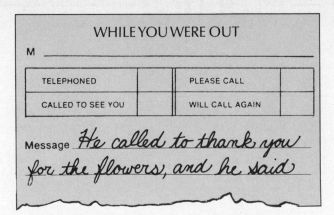

WHILE YOU WERE OUT

M _____

| TELEPHONED | PLEASE CALL |
| CALLED TO SEE YOU | WILL CALL AGAIN |

Message *He called to thank you for the flowers, and he said*

4 **Dictation**

Ken called Officer Brady to give him some important information. Listen to their conversation. Then listen again and complete it.

KEN: Officer Brady? This is Ken Wilson.
BRADY: Yes, Mr. Wilson. How can I help you?
KEN: Well, this may sound crazy, but . . .
BRADY: Yes?
KEN: Well, _____ Frank Jordan's assistant, Carol Fullerton, and . . .

BRADY: Yes, go on.
KEN: Well, _____ .
BRADY: Are you sure?
KEN: Yes, _____ .
BRADY: Do you know her?
KEN: No, but _____ .

What important information did Ken give Officer Brady? Complete these statements.

1. Ken said _____ .
2. Ken told Brady _____ .

3. Ken said _____ .
4. Ken told Brady _____ .

5 While everyone else is busy, Brad is interviewing people on the street for the *Herald's* "What's Your Opinion?" column. Read the column and report what the people said, like this:

Cindy Baker said she had been living in Houston for the past ten years. She also said . . .

The Houston Herald

What's Your Opinion?

What do you like or dislike about Houston?

Carlos Ramírez

Well, I'm from Baytown, a small town near Houston. I like it because the people are friendly, but it's not very exciting, so I'm thinking of moving to Houston.

Cindy Baker

I've been living in Houston for the past ten years, and I really love it. I especially like the nightlife. The only thing I don't like is the weather. It's too hot and humid.

Betsy Carson

I've lived in Houston all my life, and I'm going to live in Houston forever. I love the weather because I can swim almost all year round. And the people are the best I've ever met.

6 **Now ask some classmates how they feel about where they live. Take notes and then report their answers to the class.**

A: What do you like about *Toronto?*
B: I like *the excitement.*
A: What do you dislike about *Toronto?*
B: . . .

A: *Maria* said *she* liked *the excitement in Toronto. She said* . . .

B.

He asked,	"Where is she?" "When is she leaving?" "Are you sure?" "Have you met her?" "Will you tell me her address?"	He asked	where **she was.** when **she was leaving.** if **I* was** sure. if **I* had met** her. if **I* would tell** him* her address.

*Note the pronoun changes.

1 **Report the questions.**

1. CATHY: Where's Linda?
   MINH: I don't know. Can you figure out her message?

Cathy asked where Linda was. Minh asked . . .

2. CATHY: Have you heard from Linda?
   BRAD: No. What's wrong?

3. TOM: What are we going to do?
   PETE: I don't know. Will the police be able to find her?

2 **Officer Brady called Frank at home to ask him questions about Carol. Read their conversation.**

BRADY: How long has Carol Fullerton worked for you?
FRANK: About six months.
BRADY: Is she from Houston?
FRANK: No, she isn't. She's from Austin.
BRADY: Have you seen her today?
FRANK: No, I haven't. Why do you ask?
BRADY: I called her home, and she wasn't there. Where is she?
FRANK: She's in Austin. Her mother's sick.
BRADY: Can I have her phone number there?
FRANK: I'm sorry. I don't have it.
BRADY: When will she be back?
FRANK: She said she'd be back in a few days.

Now Frank is talking on the phone to Angela. Continue their conversation by reporting the five other questions that Officer Brady asked.

FRANK: Officer Brady called and asked me a lot of questions about Carol.
ANGELA: Like what?
FRANK: He asked me how long she had worked for me.
ANGELA: What else did he ask?
FRANK: He asked . . .

3 Find out if your classmate has ever been asked an embarrassing question.

A: Has anyone ever asked you an embarrassing question?

B: Yes. One time *someone* asked me *how much money I made.*

A: What did you say?

B: I said *I'd rather not say.*

Student B can use these ideas:

What's your religion?	Why don't you have
How much do you	children?
weigh?	Why aren't you married?
How old are you?	. . .

Carol **told** Phil	**to get** the truck.
	not to use the front door.

4 Review and Build

Carol, Luke and Phil are almost ready to leave. Read the conversation and report the commands, like this:

Linda told Luke not to tie her hands too tight.

LINDA: Don't tie my hands too tight.

CAROL: Phil, go get the truck. Don't use the front door.

PHIL: Luke, carry the crate to the truck. Linda, don't make any noise.

LUKE: Carol, help me get her into the crate. Hurry and leave, Phil.

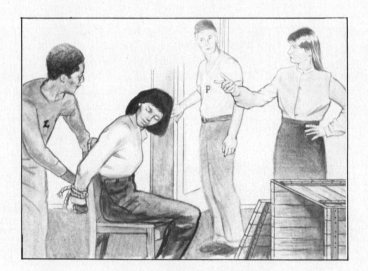

PUT IT ALL TOGETHER

Cathy and Minh are telling Officer Brady about Linda's strange telephone call. Listen and complete their conversation.

BRADY: This does sound strange. Go on. Tell me everything you can remember.

MINH: Well, Linda said she couldn't meet Angela at some restaurant because she _had_ ₁ _to_ ₂ see her sister.

CATHY: Didn't she also say what time she ___ ₃ ___ ₄ ___ ₅ meet Angela and the name of the restaurant?

MINH: Yes. She said she was going to meet Angela at ___ ₆. But I didn't really understand the name of the restaurant.

CATHY: Try to remember. This is important.

MINH: It was a ___ ₇ name. Something like "fwaygo."

BRADY: That sounds like ___ ₈.

CATHY: Yes, and I think Linda studied Spanish. Let's ___ ₉ it ___ ₁₀ in the dictionary.

BRADY: I don't know what it ___ ₁₁, but I think it's spelled ___–___–___–___–___ ₁₂. Here, I found it! Aha! I think I know what Linda meant. We'd better get going!

CATHY: OK. Let me leave a message for Pete and Tom.

Now look at the dictionary page and think about what Linda said. Why did Linda:

1. mention 6:00?
2. name the restaurant El Fuego?

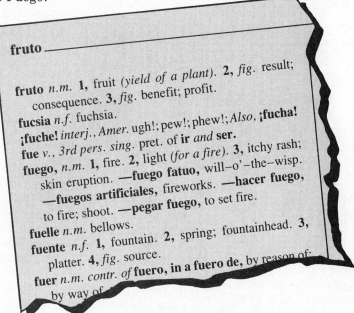

fruto

fruto *n.m.* **1,** fruit (*yield of a plant*). **2,** *fig.* result; consequence. **3,** *fig.* benefit; profit.

fucsia *n.f.* fuchsia.

¡fuche! *interj., Amer.* ugh!; pew!; phew!; *Also,* **¡fucha!**

fue *v., 3rd pers. sing.* pret. of **ir** *and* **ser.**

fuego, *n.m.* **1,** fire. **2,** light (*for a fire*). **3,** itchy rash; skin eruption. **—fuego fatuo,** will-o'-the-wisp. **—fuegos artificiales,** fireworks. **—hacer fuego,** to fire; shoot. **—pegar fuego,** to set fire.

fuelle *n.m.* bellows.

fuente *n.f.* **1,** fountain. **2,** spring; fountainhead. **3,** platter. **4,** *fig.* source.

fuer *n.m. contr. of* **fuero, in a fuero de,** by reason of; by way of.

Complete Cathy's message for Pete and Tom. (The message is printed upside down below.)

Dear Pete and Tom,

We've gone to find Linda. Meet us at _____.

_____

Cathy

Meet us at Warehouse 6.

ON YOUR OWN
Think of Brad's interview for the *Herald's* "What's Your Opinion?" column on page 96. Then discuss these questions with your classmates.

1 What do you like or dislike about the city or town you are now living in?

2 What did you like or dislike about the city or town you grew up in?

Reading

An editorial is a newspaper article in which the editor of the newspaper gives his or her opinion about important issues.

1 Predicting. Look quickly at this editorial. What issue does it discuss?

The Houston Herald

AN ANTI-SMOKING BILL

The state legislature is considering a bill that would make it illegal to smoke in government offices. The bill was (5) proposed by state legislator Tom Ortega and has the support of the many other representatives, as well as of numerous lobbying groups such (10) as the Citizens for Clean Air and the Lung Association. Those who support the measure say that secondhand smoke—smoke that you inhale while you are (15) near a smoker—may cause lung cancer in nonsmokers. In addition, they say that everyone has the right to work in a smoke-free environment. Those (20) opposed to the bill say that people have a right to smoke and no one has ever proven that secondhand smoke can cause cancer.

(25)   We agree with the bill's supporters. Smoking has been shown to be a health hazard. In our opinion, even if there is no scientific proof yet that (30) secondhand smoke causes cancer, there is no reason why nonsmokers should be forced to take this risk. If the bill is passed, workers in government (35) offices will have to either quit smoking at work or quit their jobs. We think that those who choose to quit smoking will be grateful for this bill. It may (40) save their lives.

2 Comprehension. Now read the article and answer the questions.

1. What does the anti-smoking bill say?
2. Who supports the anti-smoking bill?
3. Why do the bill's supporters think the bill should be made law?
4. Why do some people believe that the bill should not be passed?
5. Who does the editor agree with?
6. If the bill passes, what will the government workers have to do?

3 Separating facts from opinion. Read these statements. According to the editorial, which ones are facts and which ones are opinions?

1. Tom Ortega supports the anti-smoking bill.
2. The anti-smoking bill would make smoking in government offices illegal.
3. The Citizens for Clean Air support the bill.
4. Secondhand smoke is dangerous.
5. People have a right to smoke.
6. If the bill is passed, smokers will not be able to smoke while they work in government offices.
7. The anti-smoking bill may save people's lives.

4 Discussion. What do you think? Discuss this question with your classmates.

Do you think smoking in public places should be illegal? Why or why not?

Writing

Skill: Stating an opinion
Task: Writing a letter

1   A newspaper editorial is usually written in this way:

1. statement of the problem
2. arguments on both sides of the problem
3. statement of the editor's opinion
4. reasons for the editor's opinion

Reread the editorial on page 100. Find sentences that are examples of each of the four parts above.

2   Look at the editorial again. Find the three phrases that introduce the editor's opinion.

1. We agree   2.   3.

3   Write a letter to the editor of a newspaper, either agreeing or disagreeing with the editorial on smoking. Before you write, list the reasons for your opinion. Try to use the phrases that you listed in Exercise 2, but remember to change the pronouns from *we* to *I* and from *our* to *my*.

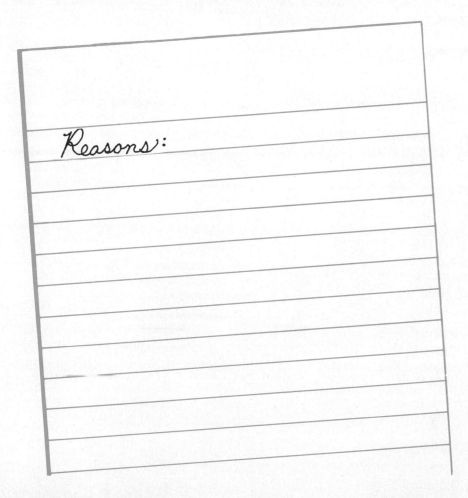

Reasons:

For pronunciation exercises for Unit 11, see page 116.

1 Listen to this article from the *Herald*.

The Houston Herald

Arsonists Arrested, Reporter Rescued

HOUSTON—After a dramatic shootout last night, Houston police arrested two men and a woman who they believe are responsible for five warehouse fires in the Houston area.

The drama began when the police received information that the three were planning to burn down Warehouse 6 on Palmer Road. When the police arrived at the scene, they found the trio removing a large crate from a truck. When the police tried to question them, the two men started shooting and a ten-minute gun battle began. It ended when the gunmen ran out of ammunition and the police made them surrender. No one was hurt, but when the police opened the crate, they found *Herald* reporter Linda Smith inside. The arsonists took Ms. Smith prisoner after she discovered their apartment hideout. Arrested on charges of arson, robbery, kidnapping and attempted murder were Carol Fullerton, 28, Luke Davis, 35, and Phil Watts, 32, all of Houston.

According to police detective George Brady, the arsonists' motive was robbery. Before they set fire to Warehouse 5 last week, they stole a group of priceless paintings which the Houston Art Museum was storing there. The robbers then replaced the valuable art with worthless paintings and burned down the warehouse so that no one would discover the robbery. All the other fires were started so that the police would not pay special attention to the fire in Warehouse 5 where the art was originally.

The arsonists say that they were hired by wealthy art collector Evans Collier, who was going to buy the paintings from them. Mr. Collier's lawyer would not let him speak to the press. His lawyer said, however, that Mr. Collier knew nothing of the arsonists or their plans.

Herald reporter, Tom Kirby, who was present at the scene, said that Ms. Smith had called the newspaper with a secret message that told of the arsonists' deadly plans. Part of that message was in Spanish. "Linda always thought her Spanish was bad. She didn't know that one day it was going to help save her life."

Officer Brady also said, "Ms. Smith was very helpful to the police. She ought to get a medal for bravery."

2 Put these events in order.

a. ____ The police found Linda.
b. ____ Luke and Phil started to shoot.
c. ____ The police arrived at Warehouse 6.
d. ____ The police arrested Luke, Phil and Carol.
e. _1_ The arsonists arrived at Warehouse 6.
f. ____ The arsonists told the police about Evans Collier.
g. ____ The police tried to talk to the arsonists.
h. ____ Luke and Phil ran out of ammunition.

3 Find a word or phrase in the article that means:

1. give up
2. a gunfight
3. three people
4. newspaper reporters
5. a reason for doing something

Practice

A.

> Carol **was going to be** a scientist, but that never happened.

1 Carol is thinking about her life. Look at the pictures and say what she thought her life was going to be like.

1. Carol was going to be a scientist.

2

3

4

5

2 Talk about what you thought your English class was going to be like before it began.

A: I thought the class was going to be *very difficult.*
B: I thought I was going to *have a lot of problems understanding the teacher.*

3 Review and Build

Can you remember the story? Did these people do these things? Make statements using *was/were going to* or the past tense. Do not use any negatives.

1. Carol / sell the paintings
Carol was going to sell the paintings, but she didn't.
2. Carol / steal the paintings
Carol stole the paintings.
3. Luke, Phil and Carol / kill Linda
4. Linda / find the arsonists

5. Phil / buy a new car
6. Luke / put Linda in a crate
7. Carol, Phil and Luke / leave the U.S.
8. An art collector / buy the paintings
9. Officer Brady and Cathy / rescue Linda
10. Luke, Phil and Carol / burn down Warehouse 5

B.

> Angela **let** Linda **stay** with her.
> Linda **didn't let** the anonymous letter **frighten** her.
> Carol **made** Linda **sit** in a chair.

1 Tell what the criminals *let* and *made* Linda do.

1. They made her sit in a chair.

1

2

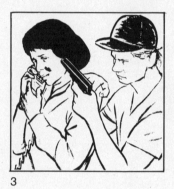
3

4

5

2 Listen to the conversation Pete and Michael had yesterday. Then look at the list and decide if Pete *let*, *didn't let* or *made* Michael do the following things.

	Let	Didn't let	Made
1. go out and play	✓		
2. call his grandmother			
3. drink a glass of soda			
4. drink a glass of chocolate milk			
5. have cookies			
6. invite a friend to dinner			
7. do his homework before dinner			
8. do his homework with a friend			

Now ask and answer questions like this about Pete and Michael.

A: Did Michael want to go out and play?
B: Yes, and Pete let him.

A: Did Michael want to call his grandmother?
B: No, but Pete made him.

3 Talk about your childhood.

A: Did your *parents let* you *stay up late* when you were a child?

B: Yes, *they* did.

OR   No, *they made* me *go to bed before 8:00.*

Student A can use these ideas:

study a lot	wear make-up
clean the house	eat food you didn't like
stay home alone	go on dates
go to the movies with your friends	take care of your brothers and sisters

C.

> They **ought to give** Linda a medal.

Note: *Ought to* means *should*. It is not usually used in questions or negative statements.

1 Some of the *Herald* staff is talking about Linda. Listen to the conversation and choose the things they say they ought to do for her.

1. buy her a present
2. take her out to dinner
3. have a party for her
4. give her a trophy
5. give her a raise

2 Pete is planning a surprise party for Linda. He can only invite ten people in addition to Linda, Michael and himself.

Look at this list of possible guests. Who do you think he ought to invite? Who don't you think he ought to invite? Why?

A: I don't think he ought to invite *Johnny and Ellen Wilson. They're too young.*

B: I agree.

OR   Oh, I think he ought to invite *them. Linda seems close to Cathy and her kids.*

Angela Lentini Cathy Wilson
Frank Jordan Ken Wilson
Suzanne Steve Wilson
Alice Thomas Ellen Wilson
Bill Thomas Johnny Wilson
Officer Brady Tom Kirby
Brad Kimball Chief of the Fire
Minh Tran Department
Lan Tran

3 What do you think ought to happen to these people in the story?

1. A: I think they ought to give Linda a medal.
   B: I think she ought to . . .

1

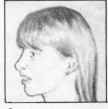
2

3

4

5

6

7

Just for Fun

4 Complete this crossword puzzle.

The *Herald* Crossword Puzzle

Across

1. Where the arsonists will probably go
4. Officer Brady works for them
7. Opposite of *off*
8. Can you tell me what time ____ is?
9. Be good ____ doing something
11. Opposite of *interested*
12. I think ____ .
13. Find necessary
15. Biggest city in the U.S. (abbreviation)
16. Person who starts fires
22. Have you done it ____?
23. She's lived here ____ 1986.
24. Look it ____ in the dictionary.
25. They take care of ____ other.
28. One time
31. Your and my
33. You and I
34. Home of the *Herald*
35. He hurt ____self.
36. His and hers
37. Opposite of *dark*

Down

1. Boy's name
2. ____ informant gives information.
3. She found the arsonists
4. What Minh Tran takes
5. Not tell the truth
6. Opposite of *hard*
10. Ought ____
14. We see with them
17. Linda Smith's profession
18. ____ to meet you.
19. Be interested ____ something
20. Location
21. Kind of drink
26. Motorcyclist's hat
27. As quiet as a ____
29. Isn't able to
30. I don't know ____ to do.
32. You and me
33. Good (adverb)
35. Embrace

Life Skills

Employment

1 **Ken Wilson is going to start working as a welder at one of Frank Jordan's businesses—Jordan Ironworks. Ken is asking his supervisor, Allan, some questions about company benefits. Listen and complete their conversation.**

KEN: I've got some questions about company _benefits_ .
                                     1

ALLAN: Sure. What would you like to know?

KEN: Well, first of all, I'd like to know about ____ ____ .
                                          2   3

ALLAN: You get major medical health insurance, which helps cover your ____ visits and your
                                                                           4

            ____ bills. You don't get dental coverage, though.
            5

KEN: Does the major medical ____ immediately?
                                    6

ALLAN: No. It starts after you've been here for ____ ____ .
                                               7   8

KEN: And what about life ____? I've got a wife and two kids.
                         9

ALLAN: You also get that after three months on the ____ . And you get disability.
                                                        10

KEN: And how much ____ time do I get?
                        11

ALLAN: ____ ____ after a ____ , ____ weeks after ____ years, and ____ weeks after
        12   13   14   15   16   17

       ____ years.
       18

KEN: That doesn't sound bad.

ALLAN: Yeah, we've got a pretty good union here.

Now ask and answer questions about someone's job benefits, like this:

A: Does your wife get health insurance?
B: Yes, she does. She gets Blue Cross/Blue Shield. OR No, she doesn't.

2 **Ken is talking to another worker at Jordan's Ironworks. He's asking him some questions about company rules. Look at the pictures and ask and answer questions with *let* or *make*.**

1. A: Do they make you punch in and out?
   B: Yes, they do.

1. punch in and out

2. take breaks

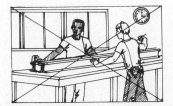
3. listen to music

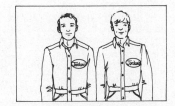
4. wear a uniform

5. smoke on the job

6. work overtime

Now ask and answer questions about someone's job. Use the ideas in the pictures above.

For Your Information

Paycheck deductions

When you receive a paycheck, there will usually be several deductions. Money for health insurance (MED), unemployment compensation (UC) and disability compensation (DC) is taken out of your total (gross) earnings. Union dues may also be deducted. A percentage of your earnings is deducted for federal income taxes and for social security (FICA). Some states and cities also have taxes. The money that is left after deductions is your take-home pay (net pay).

3 **Ken has received his first paycheck. Look at his paycheck stub and then complete the sentences.**

EMPLOYEE NAME		PERIOD		
Ken Wilson		Week		

EMPLOYEE NUMBER	SOCIAL SECURITY NO.	PERIOD ENDING
080111-0670	555-01-9011	8-7-90

THIS PAY PERIOD EARNINGS			DEDUCTIONS AND ADJUSTMENTS				OTHER PAY INFORMATION
TYPE	HOURS/UNITS	AMOUNT	TYPE	AMOUNT	TYPE	AMOUNT	
REG @ $16	40	640 00	UC	5 66			
OT @ $24	4	96 00	DC	9 00			
			UNION	8 00			

DESCRIPTION	THIS PAY	YEAR TO DATE
EARNINGS	736 00	736 00
FED. INCOME TAX	144 80	144 80
FICA	50 68	50 68
STATE TAX		
LOCAL TAX		
OTHER TAX		
DED/ADJ	22 66	
NET PAY	517 86	

STATEMENT OF EARNINGS & DEDUCTIONS
DETACH AND RETAIN FOR YOUR RECORDS

DEPOSITED TEXAS SAVINGS BANK

1. Ken gets paid _once a week_ .
   once a month / once a week / every two weeks
2. Ken worked _____ hours this week.
   40 / 44 / 16
3. Ken's overtime pay is _____ his regular pay.
   two times / the same as / one and a half times
4. Ken's gross earnings are _____.
   $736.00 / $16.00 / $517.86
5. Ken's year-to-date earnings are _____ his earnings for this pay period.
   the same as / more than / less than
6. In Ken's next check, his year-to-date earnings will be _____ his earnings for the pay period.
   the same as / more than / less than
7. If you work in Houston, you have to pay
   _____ .
   local, state and federal taxes / state and federal taxes / federal tax only

ON YOUR OWN
Discuss these questions with your classmates.

1 What kinds of job benefits do you think are important?

2 Do you think everyone should have the same job benefits? If not, what should they depend on (length of time at the job, age, ability, need)?

3 How much vacation time do you think people should get?

4 What job benefits do people get in your country? How much vacation time do they get?

For pronunciation exercises for Unit 12, see page 116.

REVIEW 6

1 Change these statements to reported speech.

1. Linda said, "I want some water."

Linda said she wanted some water.

2. Carol said, "We have to hurry."
3. Pete said, "Linda's in trouble."
4. Minh said, "I can't understand her message."
5. Angela said, "I won't be back until Tuesday."

2 Change these questions to reported speech.

1. Angela asked, "Where's the Lewis file?"

Angela asked where the Lewis file was.

2. Linda asked, "Can you untie my hands?"
3. Pete asked, "Have you done your homework, Michael?"
4. Minh asked, "Will the police find Linda?"
5. Cathy asked, "When's Officer Brady coming?"

3 Angela is in Dallas. She called the *Herald*. Read the conversation she had with Minh.

ANGELA: Hello, Minh. Is Linda there?
MINH: No, she isn't.
ANGELA: Where is she?
MINH: No one knows. She's missing. She called earlier and gave me a message, but I can't understand it. Actually, I'm sure she's in trouble.
ANGELA: Have you called the police?
MINH: Yes.
ANGELA: Well, I'm coming back right now.

Next Angela called her husband, Frank. Complete the message she left on his answering machine.

I have to come back to Houston immediately. I just called and spoke to Minh. He said that

Linda ___*was*___ missing. She called the *Herald* and left a message, but he said he
   1. be

_____ it. He said she _____ in trouble. He told me that they _____ the police,
2. can understand–neg.   3. be   4. call

but I think I should be there. I told him that I _____ back right away. I'll see you tonight.
                                             5. come

4 Change these commands to reported speech.

1. Cathy said, "Be quiet, kids."

Cathy told the kids to be quiet.

2. Ken said, "Don't stay up late, children."

Ken told the children not to stay up late.

3. Pete said, "Do your homework, Michael."
4. Angela said, "Get me the Lewis file, Brad."

5. Suzanne said, "Don't forget to write me a letter, Pete."
6. Lan said, "Call me before 6:00, Minh."
7. Carol said, "Hurry up, Luke."
8. Luke said, "Don't make so much noise, Phil."
9. Officer Brady said, "Tell me everything, Mr. Jordan."

5 Read Pete's letter to Suzanne. Change the underlined words to direct speech.

1. Angela said, "Take a vacation, Linda."

\\\

Dear Suzanne,

　　I'm sure you've heard about all the excitement we've had here. Luckily everything's OK now. Linda had a rough time, and (1) Angela told her to take a vacation. But (2) Linda said that she was fine. (3) She told us she just wanted to get back to work. That woman is amazing!

　　Guess what! Frank Jordan is looking for a new assistant. (4) Angela asked me if I knew anyone who had a background in art. (5) I told her that I knew someone who might be interested. It's really the perfect job for you, Suzanne. (6) Angela said to tell you to send Frank a résumé as soon as possible.

6 When you were a child, what did you decide you were going to do when you grew up? Write five sentences.

EXAMPLE: When I was a child, I decided I was going to be an engineer.

7 Write sentences about what parents *should let, shouldn't let* and *should make* their children do.

1. eat good meals

Parents should make their children eat good meals.

2. stay up late
3. go out with their friends sometimes
4. drink a lot of soda
5. be polite to adults
6. watch too much TV
7. make some of their own decisions
8. do their homework
9. have fun

8 Your friends want to improve their English. Tell them five things that they *ought to* do. You can choose from the list below or make your own suggestions.

take English classes
read the dictionary
listen to the radio
be quiet in class
make friends with some Americans
read English newspapers
speak correctly all the time
buy lots of grammar review books
go to English movies
ask questions when they don't understand
speak English as much as possible
memorize the alphabet
ask their friends to translate for them

Pronunciation

The Pronunciation exercises are recorded on cassette after the listening exercises for each unit. The Tapescripts are found at the back of the Teacher's Manual.

UNIT 1

Part 1

Listen and complete these sentences.

1. Tom _____ _____ _____ .
2. He doesn't like _____ .
3. He _____ to use a typewriter.
4. Linda usually _____ _____ about _____ .
5. Now _____ doing a story about all _____ _____ _____ .

Now listen again and repeat the sentences.

Part 2

Listen to these sentences and complete each one with the correct object pronoun.

1. Look _____ up in the dictionary.
2. Why don't you call _____ up?
3. Drop _____ off at the library.
4. Pete's handing _____ in.
5. Yes, do _____ over.
6. Please point _____ out to me.

Now listen again and repeat the sentences.

Part 3

Listen to these sentences and mark the word that has the *most* stress in each sentence.

Example: I think it's right.

1. Well, I think so.
2. But you speak Spanish.
3. It's very difficult.
4. I won't understand anything.

Now listen again and repeat the sentences.

UNIT 2

Part 1

Linda is talking to her new neighbor, Vicky. Listen to their conversation and complete it.

VICKY: How long _____ you _____ in Houston, Linda?
1 2

LINDA: Oh, _____ _____ here all my life. I was
3 4
_____ in Houston. What about you?
5

VICKY: We _____ to Texas in _____ _____
6 7 8
I got a _____ job here.
9

LINDA: _____ the way, _____ you met _____
10 11 12
and Alice? They _____ in apartment
13
2_____ .
14

VICKY: Yes. They seem _____ nice.
15

Now listen again and repeat the conversation.

Part 2

Listen to these sentences and complete them with *has, hasn't, have* or *haven't*.

1. Alice _____ seen Bill.
2. The doctors _____ examined him.
3. _____ he woken up?
4. The police _____ found the driver.
5. Alice _____ called her sister.

Now listen again and repeat the sentences.

Part 3

Listen to these questions and mark the word that has the *most* stress in each question.

1. Why didn't you call the police?
2. Why didn't you call the police?

Now listen again and match the questions with these answers.

a. Because Minh already called them.
b. Because I thought it was a job for the fire department.

UNIT 3

Part 1

A. Listen to these verbs in the present and past tenses. How many syllables do you hear—1, 2 or 3?

	Present	Syllables		Past	Syllables		
Ex.:	connect	1 (2)		connected	1 2 (3)		
1.	try	1 2		tried	1 2 3		
2.	use	1 2		used	1 2 3		
3.	protect	1 2		protected	1 2 3		
4.	finish	1 2		finished	1 2 3		
5.	visit	1 2		visited	1 2 3		
6.	need	1 2		needed	1 2 3		
7.	talk	1 2		talked	1 2 3		
8.	work	1 2		worked	1 2 3		
9.	hate	1 2		hated	1 2 3		
10.	happen	1 2		happened	1 2 3		
11.	start	1 2		started	1 2 3		
12.	want	1 2		wanted	1 2 3		

Now listen again and repeat each word.

B. 1. Which words in Exercise A have the same number of syllables in the present and in the past?

_____

_____

2. Which words in Exercise A have *more* syllables in the past than in the present?

_____

_____

Note that these words end in a *t* or *d* sound in the present tense.

C. Listen and repeat this conversation.

A: What did you do yesterday?
B: I visited my aunt. She wanted me to help her paint her bedroom.
A: What did you do after you painted the room?
B: Oh, we just talked about people we used to know.

Part 2

Listen and repeat these sentences. Notice that *used to* and *use to* are pronounced the same way.

1. Angela used to live in Toronto.
2. Pete used to be married.
3. Tom didn't use to speak Spanish.
4. Did Linda use to paint?
5. Minh didn't use to ride a motorcycle.

UNIT 4

Part 1

Steve Wilson is talking to his friend Bob. Listen to their conversation and complete it.

BOB: What's the _____ ?
                         1
STEVE: My _____ can't find a job.
              2
BOB: He's a good _____ . Where's he been
                         3
looking?

STEVE: He looks in the _____ every day.
                              4
BOB: I _____ when I was unemployed. It's hard,
         5
but I'm sure he'll find _____ job soon.
                              6

Now listen again and repeat the conversation.

Part 2

Listen to these sentences and complete them with *can* or *can't*.

1. We _____ go to the movies.
2. Johnny _____ play outside.
3. You _____ find a job.
4. They _____ stop at the store.
5. The Wilsons _____ spend a lot of money.

Now listen again and repeat the sentences.

Part 3

Listen to these sentences. Notice the difference in pronunciation between stressed *too* and unstressed *to*.

1. It's tóo hot to drink.
2. They're tóo tired to work.
3. She's tóo yóung to vóte.
4. It's tóo expénsive to búy.
5. I'm tóo búsy to tálk.

Now listen again and repeat the sentences.

UNIT 5

Part 1

Listen and complete these sentences.

1. I'm not _____ anywhere.
2. Two heads are _____ than one.
3. Johnny's _____ .
4. They're _____ to each other.
5. She can't read the _____ .

Now listen again and repeat the sentences.

(continued)

Part 2

Listen and complete each sentence with the adjective you hear.

1. She's very _____.
   interesting/interested

2. He's _____.
   exciting/excited

3. They're not _____.
   frightening/frightened

4. He's _____.
   tiring/tired

5. Is she _____?
   boring/bored

Now listen again and repeat the sentences.

Part 3

Sometimes an unstressed syllable is reduced so much it disappears. Listen to these sentences and cross out the vowel that you *don't* hear in each underlined word.

Example: The movie was fright~~e~~ning.

1. I thought the book was interesting.
2. Bill's studying business.
3. Let's do something different.
4. That's Minh's best camera.

Now listen again and repeat the sentences.

UNIT 6

Part 1

Pete and Tom are talking about Linda. Listen to their conversation and complete it.

PETE: I'm really _____ about Linda.
       1

TOM: I know. She always _____ too hard.
     2

PETE: No, it's not that. I'm _____ about that letter
      3

she got when she _____ to the office today.
                  4

TOM: Oh, I _____ about that. What does Officer
     5

Brady think?

PETE: I don't know. But I'm _____ . I don't want
      6

Linda to get _____ .
             7

Now listen again and repeat the conversation.

Part 2

Listen to these sentences. Notice how the voice rises and then falls in the *if-* clause.

1. If Pete finds an apartment, he'll move.
2. If Ken gets a job, he'll be happy.
3. If Michael doesn't study, he won't pass.
4. If Cathy calls, I'll tell you.
5. If Linda isn't careful, she'll get hurt.

Now listen again and repeat the sentences.

Part 3

A. Listen and repeat these *yes/no* questions. Remember that your voice goes up at the end.

1. Have you seen Linda?
2. Are you enjoying working in Houston?
3. Can I take a message?
4. Could I have the day off?

B. Now listen and repeat these *wh-* questions. Remember that your voice goes down at the end.

1. Who sent it?   3. What's the matter?
2. What's it about?   4. Where's Linda?

UNIT 7

Part 1

Listen and complete these sentences.

1. Linda's _____ a special _____ .
2. _____ is _____ .
3. Linda's _____ isn't always _____ .
4. She _____ a _____ letter.
5. Angela doesn't _____ mentioning the _____ .

Now listen again and repeat the sentences.

Part 2

A. When we speak quickly, the word *and* is sometimes pronounced *n* and the word *or* is sometimes pronounced *er*. Listen and repeat these phrases.

1. Linda and Carol
2. Cathy and Ken
3. writing about politics and investigating crimes
4. a couple of people at the paper and the police
5. an editor or a social worker
6. painting or reading
7. Wisconsin or Kansas
8. oranges or grapes

B. Now listen to these sentences and complete them with *and* or *or*.

1. She writes about politics _____ crime.
2. We can celebrate tomorrow _____ Saturday.
3. Let's invite Frank _____ Angela.
4. Cathy likes jogging _____ bicycling.
5. I think corn is grown in Kansas _____ Illinois.
6. I'd like apple pie _____ ice cream, please.

Now listen again and repeat the sentences.

Part 3

Listen to these sentences. Put a period after each statement and a question mark after each question.

1. a. She's here _____   b. She's here _____
2. a. Routine _____   b. Routine _____
3. a. They're eating _____   b. They're eating _____
4. a. It's 10 o'clock _____   b. It's 10 o'clock _____
5. a. He's not sure _____   b. He's not sure _____

Now listen again and repeat the sentences.

UNIT 8

Part 1

A. Listen and complete these sentences.

1. Ken works the night _____ .
2. Are you _____ ?
3. Don't _____ this to anyone.
4. You _____ go alone.
5. Can you repeat the _____ ?
6. Rob has to go to _____ and Save.

Now listen again and repeat the sentences.

B. Listen to this tongue twister and repeat it as fast as you can. How many times can you say it without making a mistake?

She sells seashells by the seashore.

Part 2

Listen and complete each sentence with the verb you hear.

1. Ken _____ hired after Christmas.
   was/wasn't
2. Bill _____ arrested last year.
   was/wasn't
3. The doors _____ locked at 6:00.
   are/aren't
4. Rice _____ grown in Arkansas.
   is/isn't
5. Paychecks _____ given out every week.
   are/aren't

Now listen again and repeat the sentences.

Part 3

Listen to these sentences. Notice the rising and then the falling intonation in the clause with the time expression *(when, as soon as, after* or *before)*.

1. When Rob leaves, he'll go home.
2. As soon as I know, I'll tell you.
3. After Pete's done, he'll call Suzanne.
4. Before Linda has dinner, she'll visit Bill.
5. When I get my license, I'll buy a car.

Now listen again and repeat the sentences.

UNIT 9

Part 1

Officer Brady is talking to Ken again. Listen to their conversation and complete it.

BRADY: _____ for coming again, Mr. Wilson.
         1

KEN: Sure _____ , Officer Brady. I want to help
             2

       find _____ people.
              3

BRADY: Just tell me _____ you can remember
                        4

       about _____ fire .
              5

KEN: I _____ I already told you _____
          6   7

       whole story.

BRADY: Well, if you remember _____ else,
                               8

       please call.

KEN: I sure will. I've asked my _____ , but he
                                    9

       doesn't remember much _____ .
                               10

Now listen again and repeat the conversation.

Part 2

Listen to these sentences and complete them with *must* or *mustn't*.

1. You _____ tell her about it.
2. You _____ do it again.
3. You _____ wash it in hot water.
4. You _____ send it to the cleaners.
5. You _____ stop there.
6. She _____ work today.
7. She _____ go there alone.
8. You _____ tell him.

Now listen again and repeat the sentences.

UNIT 10

Part 1

Pete and Tom are talking about Linda again. Listen to their conversation and complete it.

PETE: Have _____ heard from Linda _____?
  ₁   ₂

TOM: _____. She called _____ a few
  ₃   ₄
minutes ago.

PETE: Where was she?

TOM: At some diner. I think that her _____
  ₅
friend Bill was there too.

PETE: I don't like this. When's _____ coming back?
  ₆

TOM: Not until _____ 18th. I hope Linda can stay
  ₇
out of trouble until then.

PETE: Yes. And I hope Bill can stay out of _____.
  ₈

Now listen again and repeat the conversation.

Part 2

Listen and complete each conversation with *should've* or *shouldn't have*.

1. A: What's the matter?
   B: I _____ watched that program.
2. A: What's wrong?
   B: I _____ bought that sweater.
3. A: What's the matter?
   B: We _____ gone on vacation.
4. A: Is something wrong?
   B: Yes. We _____ invited your sister to dinner.
5. A: Are you upset about something?
   B: Yes. You _____ told him about it.
6. A: What do *you* think?
   B: They _____ gotten married.

Now listen again and repeat each conversation.

UNIT 11

Part 1

Listen and complete these sentences.

1. I got a _____ strange _____ from _____.
2. _____? I don't _____ it.
3. _____ the _____ _____ away.
4. What _____ did she say?
5. She was going to go to a _____.
6. She's _____ with _____.
7. _____ to the _____.

Now listen again and repeat the sentences.

Part 2

Minh and Cathy are talking about Linda. Listen to their conversation and complete it by choosing the correct punctuation—an exclamation point (!) after the exclamations, a period (.) after the statements and a question mark (?) after the questions.

MINH: I got a really strange phone call __ . ? __
  ₁

CATHY: Really __ . ? __ What was strange about it __ ? ! __
  ₂   ₃

MINH: Linda wanted to talk to Angela __ ? ! __
  ₄

CATHY: You're kidding __ . ! __ What else did
  ₅
she say __ . ? __
  ₆

MINH: She said she had to take care of
her sister __ . ? __
  ₇

CATHY: Her sister __ . ! __ Linda's an only child __ . ? __

Now listen again and repeat the conversation.

UNIT 12

Part 1

Listen and complete these sentences.

1. They _____ the _____ on the _____.
2. The _____ was very _____.
3. The _____ had a _____ _____.
4. They were going to _____ to _____.
5. Now Linda can take a _____.

Now listen again and repeat the sentences.

Part 2

Listen and repeat these sentences.

1. Carol was going to be a scientist.
2. She was going to be rich and famous.
3. She was going to travel a lot.
4. She was going to sell the stolen paintings.

Part 3

Frank and Angela are talking about Carol. Listen to their conversation and complete it.

FRANK: I can't believe Carol _____ kill Linda.
  ₁

ANGELA: Well, it's true. The police _____ put her
  ₂
in jail for a long time.

FRANK: I'm _____ go see her. I _____ know why
  ₃   ₄
she did this.

ANGELA: She really _____ give you a full
  ₅
explanation.

Now listen again and repeat the conversation.

Irregular Verbs

Verb	Past Tense	Past Participle	Verb	Past Tense	Past Participle
be	was, were	been	lie	lay	lain
beat	beat	beaten	light	lit *or* lighted	lit *or* lighted
become	became	become	lose	lost	lost
begin	began	begun	make	made	made
bend	bent	bent	mean	meant	meant
bet	bet	bet	meet	met	met
bite	bit	bitten	pay	paid	paid
bleed	bled	bled	put	put	put
blow	blew	blown	read	read	read
break	broke	broken	ride	rode	ridden
bring	brought	brought	ring	rang	rung
build	built	built	rise	rose	risen
burst	burst	burst	run	ran	run
buy	bought	bought	say	said	said
catch	caught	caught	see	saw	seen
choose	chose	chosen	sell	sold	sold
come	came	come	send	sent	sent
cost	cost	cost	set	set	set
cut	cut	cut	shake	shook	shaken
dive	dove	dived	shoot	shot	shot
do	did	done	shut	shut	shut
draw	drew	drawn	sing	sang	sung
drink	drank	drunk	sink	sank	sunk
drive	drove	driven	sit	sat	sat
eat	ate	eaten	sleep	slept	slept
fall	fell	fallen	slide	slid	slid
feed	fed	fed	speak	spoke	spoken
feel	felt	felt	spend	spent	spent
find	found	found	spit	spat *or* spit	spat *or* spit
fly	flew	flown	spread	spread	spread
forget	forgot	forgotten	stand	stood	stood
forgive	forgave	forgiven	steal	stole	stolen
freeze	froze	frozen	stick	stuck	stuck
get	got	gotten	sting	stung	stung
give	gave	given	stink	stank *or* stunk	stunk
go	went	gone	sweep	swept	swept
grow	grew	grown	swim	swam	swum
have	had	had	swing	swung	swung
hear	heard	heard	take	took	taken
hide	hid	hidden	teach	taught	taught
hit	hit	hit	tear	tore	torn
hold	held	held	tell	told	told
hurt	hurt	hurt	think	thought	thought
keep	kept	kept	throw	threw	thrown
know	knew	known	understand	understood	understood
lay	laid	laid	wake	woke	woken
lead	led	led	wear	wore	worn
leave	left	left	win	won	won
lend	lent	lent	write	wrote	written
let	let	let			

Word List

The numbers after each word indicate the page number where the word first appears. An asterisk (*) indicates the word is intended for recognition only on that page.

Words active in Student's Book 1 and 2 are not included in this list.

adj = adjective; *adv* = adverb; *aux* = auxiliary verb; *C* = on cassette; *conj* = conjunction; *intrans* = intransitive verb; *n* = noun; *past part* = past participle; *prep* = preposition; *pron* = pronoun; *s past* = simple past tense; *trans* = transitive verb; *v* = verb

F

face *v* 65
facility *82
fact *100
fair *adj* (not good, not bad) 17
fallen arch 52
far: so far (= up to now) 31
fast *adv* 77
fasten *91C
feather 35
federal *108
fight *v* 27
figure out 97
fill *64
film *n* (= movie) *5
finance charge *37
find
    found *past part* 20
    find out 20
fire
    by fire 68
    fire department 66
    on fire 66
    set fire *102
firefighter 2
first of all 94
first-aid station 90
flame *68
flashlight *21
flat *adj* 65
flavor *n* *64, 82
flight
    flight attendant 58
    flight monitor *90
fluently 78
fly *v* 50
follow 84
following *adj* *37
food
    baby food 72
    frozen food 72
for
    for a change *44
    for a while 49
    prepare for 15
force *v* *100
foreigner *81
forward: look forward to 60
found *past part* *8
    lost and found (department) 91
frame *n* *86
fresh (in good condition) 72
friend: best friend 22
frightening *adj* 41
front door 98
frozen food 72
frustrated *adj* 45
full 3
    full blast *adv* *26

full of *46
funny: Don't try anything funny. *88

G

garbage 62
garment *81
gasoline *25C
gate *90
generator *21
genius 26
get
    gotten *44
    get away with it *95C
    get back (= return) *intrans* *4, 20
    get back *trans* 6
    get into trouble 23
    get out of 12
    Get well soon. *68
    get-well note *68
    I'm not getting anywhere. 40
    I've got that. (= I understand.) *80C
give
    given 62
    give birth 26
    give out *trans* 62
    give up *trans* 10
glass (material) *26
go
    go off (as a gun) 27
    go on (= continue) 76
    go out (= be extinguished) 2
good: be good at 59
gotten *44
government 100
graceful 32
grammatically 78
grape *n* 61
grateful *100
gross *adj* (= total) *108
ground *n* 90
    ground transportation 90
group *n* 100
    group of *102
grow: grown 61
guard: security guard 27
guarded *adj* (condition) 17
guilty *25C, 78
gun *102
    gun battle *102
gunfight *102
gunman *102

H

had *aux* 95
    had better 48
hairdresser 58

half: in half 65
hammering *n* *46
hand in 6
hand wash *v* 81
handful 26
handicapped *n* *82
hang 65
    hung *past part* *86C
happily 77
hard *adv* 49
haven *82
hazard *n* *100
head: Two heads are better than one. 40
hear: heard *s past* *58
heart disease 17
heartily *82
heat wave 28
heavy (greater than usual) 26
hectic 35
helmet 15
hemorrhaging *n* 17
herself 43
hideout *102
himself 43
hire 66
hit *past part* 10
    s past 20
hit-and-run 20
hold *v* 65
    hold down 15
    hold on (on the phone) 55
hole 36
home: back home *8
homemade *81
hometown 47
hospitalization *17
hour
    lunch hour *14
    office hours *80C
    visiting hours 16
how *conj* 29
How do you do? 2
how much *pron* 79
however *8, 9
huge 35
humid 96
hung *past part* *86C
hurry *v* 95

I

iced tea 65
if 2
igloo *69
illegal 100
immediate 77
immediately 48
immigrate *8, 9
impolite 77
impolitely 77
improve 15

in
    break in *trans* (enter illegally) *62
    hand in 6
    in addition to *68
    in half 65
    in line 27
    in spite of *82
    in town 13
    punch in 107
    put in (= insert) *80C
income 40
    income tax 40
incorrect 77
indoor *65
industry 88
inexpensive 28
informant 10
information 10
    information booth 91
ingredient 80
ingrown toenail 52
inhale 100
injure *7, 68
injury *68
inquiry *37
inside out 81
insomnia 52
instead 28
institute *12
insurance: life insurance 107
intensive care (unit) 17
interested *adj* 41
internist 52
introduce 2
investigate 50
investigation *78
involved *adj* 76
ironing *n* *81

J

jalapeño *82
join *trans* 32
joke *v* 94
journal (= diary) 29
journalism 13
jump *n* *7C
just *adv*
    just a moment *42C
    just as 26

K

keep (have for some time) *53
    kept *past part* 62
    keep busy *30
    keep on (= continue) 59
kid: poor kid *12C
kidnap *102
kidney 52
    kidney stone 52

___ Acknowledgements _____

We wish to thank the following for providing us with photographs:

Page 15, Photos by Heinz Paul Piper. **Page 34,** *left to right: top row:* N.Y. Convention and Visitors Bureau; Photo #126–AS–5255 from The National Archives; *second row:* The Greater Houston Convention and Visitors Bureau; The Houston Post photo; *third row:* Eastman Kodak Co.; Canon U.S.A., Inc.; *bottom row:* Courtesy of Penny Laporte. **Page 69,** *Pic 1:* The Metropolitan Museum of Art, Rogers Fund, 1949; *Pic 2:* N.Y. Convention and Visitors Bureau; *Pic 3:* Smithsonian Institution Photo No. 55019; *Pic 4:* UN Photo 152,155/John Issac; *Pic 5:* Smithsonian Institution Photo No. 72–6966; *Pic 6:* London Bridge, Lake Havasu City, Arizona; *Pic 7:* V. Brand: Barnaby's Picture Library. **Page 96,** Photos by Heinz Paul Piper.